When Necessary Use Words

Changing Lives Through Worship, Justice and Evangelism

MIKE PILAVACHI
with Liza Hoeksma

From Gospel Light
Ventura, California, U.S.A.

PUBLISHED BY REGAL BOOKS
FROM GOSPEL LIGHT
VENTURA, CALIFORNIA, U.S.A.
PRINTED IN THE U.S.A.

Regal Books is a ministry of Gospel Light, a Christian publisher dedicated to serving the local church. We believe God's vision for Gospel Light is to provide church leaders with biblical, user-friendly materials that will help them evangelize, disciple and minister to children, youth and families.

It is our prayer that this Regal book will help you discover biblical truth for your own life and help you meet the needs of others. May God richly bless you.

For a free catalog of resources from Regal Books/Gospel Light, please call your Christian supplier or contact us at 1-800-4-GOSPEL *or* www.regalbooks.com.

© 2006 Mike Pilavachi
This edition issued by special arrangement with Kingsway Publications, Lottbridge Drove, Eastbourne, East Sussex, England, BN23 6NT. Original title: *Worship, Justice, Evangelism.*

Library of Congress Cataloging-in-Publication Data
Pilavachi, Mike.
   When necessary, use words / Mike Pilavachi.
      p. cm.
   Includes bibliographical references.
   ISBN 0-8307-3814-2 (trade paper)
   1. Worship. 2. Christianity and justice. 3. Evangelistic work. I. Title.
   BV15.P55 2006
   248—dc22

                                                                    2006034785

1   2   3   4   5   6   7   8   9   10   /   10   09   08   07

For additional information, visit www.gospellightworldwide.org; write to Gospel Light Worldwide, P.O. Box 3875, Ventura, CA 93006; or send an e-mail to info@gospellight worldwide.org.

To David Westlake. Your passion for God, and the way you express it through worship, evangelism and justice, has been an amazing inspiration. Your friendship, love, correction and loyalty over many years mean the world.

Contents

ACKNOWLEDGMENTS

We would like to thank many people who have helped us in understanding the issues that are expressed in this book.

To the worship leaders with whom I have argued and discussed these issues: Matt Redman, Tim Hughes, Martyn Layzell, David Ruis, Jonny Parks and Onehundredhours. Also to J. John, Bishop Graham Cray, Andrew Croft and David Pambakian for the hours of discussion on these subjects.

We would both like to thank those who have read the manuscript and given invaluable comments: Gemma Foster, Jonno Ives, Karen Layzell, Becca Sampson and Luke Williams. With particular thanks to Craig Borlase for his timely wisdom, editing skills and encouragement, and to Daniel and Marlies Hoogteyling and Emily Vesey for sharing their experiences.

Special thanks to Martyn and Emily Layzell and Ali MacInnes for their friendship, love, encouragement and wisdom. It's a pleasure and a privilege to live life with you.

Lastly, we would like to thank the church we are a part of, where all of this is worked out: Soul Survivor Watford—we love you very much.

Love God,
Love My Neighbor

This little book is written as a result of a journey my friends and I have been on these last few years. As we have studied the Word of God and allowed Him to speak to us, we have realized that an artificial divide has been created between worship, evangelism and justice. This is a divide that has to end if we are to be a biblical people who obey God in all that we sing and say and do. These issues belong hand in hand, not like options that we pick and choose—"today I'm focusing on evangelism; maybe next week it will be justice," but working together, overlapping and impacting each other in a way I hadn't fully grasped.

I believe that worship is an event, an act: The Magi bowed down and worshiped the baby Jesus, and the 24 elders cast their crowns and worshiped before the Lion of the tribe of Judah. I believe that worship is also a way of life. To worship is to witness, and to witness is to worship. God says that if we do not feed the hungry, He will not listen to our songs, yet if we look after people's physical needs without adoring God, we are forgetting our first love. To care for the poor and to fight for justice without also bringing our thanksgiving and praise to God can and does lead to jaded exhaustion and bitterness.

I passionately believe these are important concepts for us to grasp and put into practice in our lives if we are to truly see the revival that many have been praying for so long. This is the story of my journey into God's Word and into God's world. I hope it will be yours also.

Living Without Dignity

South Africa is one of my favorite places. I love the breathtaking landscapes, the feeling of the sun on my face while standing on the sandy beaches that line the coast, the amazing wildlife, the taste of a good bunny chow (a curry that doesn't actually have anything to do with rabbits), and of course the wonderfully generous and loving people I have met there. It has also been the place where God has shared something of His heart with me in a way that I know has changed me forever.

I often visit Durban, a city on the eastern coast that demonstrates one of the biggest contrasts of any culture you'll ever see. It contains both the developed world and the developing world, the extremes of rich and poor living right on each other's doorsteps. Some people live in five-bedroom gated houses with their own swimming pools and tennis courts, while just a few miles away many children have nothing and live on the street.

I've often been told to be wary of the street kids, warned off with stories of how they steal, lie and cheat. People have told me that most of them are high on drugs, that they hang around the beaches causing a nuisance and that they are threatening the tourist industry. When I was there in February, seven street boys stopped my friends and me and asked us for money. Not wanting to give them cash, we offered to buy them some food instead, and as we waited in line for their burgers, chips and coke, we began to chat with them about how they ended up on the streets. We discovered that all of them were orphans with not a single living relative among them. Can you even imagine what that would be like—not only to lose your parents, but to have literally no one else to turn to? The youngest was 13 and the eldest just 16 years old, and they had nowhere else to go but the streets.

As they answered our questions, we could see their own questions written all over their faces: "Why are you asking all of this? What do you want from us?" They spent their days begging money from strangers. Rarely did anyone want to actually talk to them; most people just threw them some coins and left as quickly as they could. As we talked, the guys huddled close together, eyeing us suspiciously, their meals disappearing into their hungry stomachs in seconds. Something started stirring in my heart. "We'll come and see you again tomorrow," I said. They shrugged and turned away, unsure whether to believe us or not. The next day we went back and found them in the same place and hung out with them again, trying to find out more about them. We went back again and again over the week. Gradually their reservations faded as they realized that we intended them no harm and were only interested in getting to know them.

The first time we met Edwin, the youngest of the group, he was obviously high from glue sniffing, but it took me until the end of the week to pluck up the courage to ask him why he did it. His response was very matter of fact: "Because it takes away the pain." There was nothing I could say to that. I had no right to tell him that what he was doing was damaging him, because I've never known the depth of pain that drives someone to that level of self-destruction.

Eventually the boys trusted us enough to take us to their "home." It was on some wasteland that our South African friends had warned us not to go near because it was dangerous. I didn't know what to expect and felt nervous as we walked there. These young boys had made their home between two trees; it was just a cardboard box that they would climb into at night to go to sleep. It was a shocking reality compared to the comforts I took for granted. I felt sick to my stomach. But the one thing I'll never forget is what I saw on one of the branches above the box. There, swinging in the breeze, were about 20 coat hangers with absolutely nothing on them. The boys didn't have enough money to buy food, so of course there was no way they would have enough to buy a change of clothes. They'd worn the same filthy, ripped trousers and T-shirts every day we'd met them. They'd found the coat hangers discarded somewhere and they needed something that would make their cardboard box between two trees feel a little more like home, so they'd brought the hangers back and hung them proudly. That disturbing image stayed with me during the four months before we were able to go back to South Africa again.

Our second trip to South Africa, when the boys saw us, they ran up to greet us, smiling, their wariness completely gone. We wanted so much to help and had been trying to think of things we could do that would make a difference to their lives. My friend and I bought them each a pair of athletic shoes, and I can't even begin to describe their joy; they didn't have one pair of shoes between them and now they were putting on brand-new shoes. They jumped around, kicking their newly adorned feet high in the air, laughing and crying out with delight. They felt like kings, but we knew there were many more needs in their life that a pair of shoes wouldn't fix.

The next stop was the supermarket. I've never felt so rich or so privileged as I did while walking in with these young guys and knowing that the things they so desperately needed were within my grasp to give. We'd intended to buy them food but also asked if there was anything else they wanted. They looked at each other and nodded. They were all agreed: What they wanted more than anything else was the strongest deodorant and soap that money could buy. I smiled at them as they scanned the shelves trying to work out which soap would make them smell the best, but my heart was cracking.

Yes, they needed food to give sustenance to their malnourished bodies, but they also needed dignity. They knew that they smelled bad—their bodies and clothes were unwashed and uncared for—but they had no way of fixing that problem themselves. They just had to accept as a part of their lives that when they were around other people, noses would turn up accompanied by looks of disgust. With soap and deodorant that cost the equivalent of just a few dollars, they could feel human again—they could hold their heads that much higher knowing they were able to take care of their bodies.

As we left the supermarket, I noticed that Edwin wasn't wearing his shoes. I asked why and the others said that he had hurt his leg and couldn't put them on. When I saw that he was walking with a slight limp, I asked if he'd been to a doctor and they laughed. What doctor would see them? Yet another thing I had taken for granted. So we took him to the local clinic, persuading the reluctant doctor to see him. I doubt that you'll ever see anyone more excited to be seeing a doctor than Edwin. The ointment and bandage they used was like bestowing him with dignity and worth, and from that moment on I never saw him without the bandage. Even once his leg was healed he wore it like a medal, proud that he had been able to see a doctor and was worthy of medical treatment.

When the time came to say good-bye before our return to the UK, they all hugged us and asked us to come and see them again. I promised that we would be back in April and would come and find them, but it was agonizing to leave.

Most nights when I climb into my comfortable bed and pull the duvet over me, I think of those boys and wonder if they're still sleeping in the same box between the same two trees, empty coat hangers above them; and I pray they're all still alive.

I'm not telling you what we did to make us sound good, because believe me, I know that our offering was small. I believe that God changed me through meeting these guys in a way that I want to share with you, as it has been a key step on my journey of faith. Meeting my friends who lived on the street in South Africa made me realize that God's heart for the poor will impact the life of *anyone* who wants to follow Him.

"Religion" Is a Dirty Word

The church is no longer at the heart of the community. If someone is in trouble, he or she may turn to friends and family, the government or even alcohol and drugs; few would consider setting foot inside a church. While there have been encouraging signs of growth in pockets of the church, the overall number of people attending services has been declining for almost a century. God has stayed the same, and His message that has always had such a radical impact on people's lives still stands today; so what has changed? Meeting Him used to be enough to turn people's lives around and cause them to leave everything behind to follow Him, but now He is often dismissed as a charismatic political leader who died an untimely death.

Our society today seems in many ways more open to spirituality than was society in the past, but we've decreased in our understanding of true faith. "Religion" has become a dirty word that even Christians don't want to be associated with—the mark of an institution that has been at the heart of war, conflict and condemnation rather than bringing a message of hope and peace.

This has been painful to watch for those of us who want to follow God with all our hearts, who know He is "the way, the truth and the life" (John 14:6), and who want those around us to live in the same freedom and love that we are living in. Society tells us that the world has less and less room for God, and yet the pain and misery we see around us show that there is perhaps a greater need than ever for all He brings. How do we reconcile these two extremes and help people to identify with God?

People who are fully devoted to God and desire to serve Him with all they have will surely impact this generation. As I've sought God and asked Him what I can do, how I can live my life for Him and how to better reflect Him to those around me, I've come back to the words of Jesus when He was asked what the greatest commandment was. He replied, "Love the Lord your God with all your heart and with all your soul and with all your mind and with all your strength" (Mark 12:30). We can't get away from the fact that loving God and being in an intimate relationship with Him is our highest priority. It's the most precious thing we have and the most important thing we should be invested in. And it should be protected at all costs.

When Jesus highlighted the greatest commandment, He was quick to say, "The second is this: 'Love your neighbor as yourself'" (v. 31). In today's global society, we may know more about the lives of people in Africa than we do about the people who live next door to us. We live in a time when we have easy access to all sorts of information. For example, we can see TV pictures of disasters happening in India literally minutes after they have happened. Our neighbor can be on the other side of the world and yet we are called to love them as ourselves.

We've often separated our spiritual activities from our secular ones: We go to a home group—that's spiritual; we buy a pair of running shoes—that's secular. Or is it? If we do our part to ensure that the person who is making our running shoes gets a fair wage and works in reasonable conditions, isn't that an act of loving our neighbor and, therefore, a spiritual activity? God is interested in the whole of our lives and He wants access to everything so that we can make choices that better reflect Him.

We're going to explore the areas of worship, justice and evangelism as three key issues that are on God's heart. These are areas that we have often separated when, in reality, they belong together. We'll be looking at what it means to worship God with all of our life and to love Him with our whole heart; what evangelism looks like in today's culture; what God's passion for justice means for us; and how we can influence this world that seems to be in such a terrible state.

I believe that worship, evangelism and justice are close to God's heart and that they belong together. If we continue to ignore these issues, or separate them, we will continue to see a decline in the numbers of people following God, and the Church's voice will grow weaker. If we bring them back together, could it be that the Church will again be right at the heart of the community and that God will again be worshiped as He deserves?

PART 1

Worship

The Highest Priority

It may be easy to say that worship is our highest priority, but to really grasp why God is so keen on it we have to do a bit more digging around the subject. It's important for us to recognize what worship is really all about, why God instilled it as the most important thing for us to do, and what happens when we let it slip. It's also important to know what happens when we offer God genuine worship. Our ultimate role model of how to give God the worship He requires is Jesus, and we need to fully grasp just what Jesus' worship looked like in order to see how ours should follow. If we assume that God will be pleased if we just sing a few worship songs, we will miss out on so much of God's blessing.

To understand the heart of worship, we have to go back to the beginning and look at the story of God's creating human life. God is love, and therefore He created us out of love. When He formed Adam and Eve, He created them to live alongside Him in the Garden of Eden. It was only when they sinned that Adam and Eve became separated from Him as we are today. When they took the fruit of the knowledge of good and evil, the heart of their sin made them want to be independent. God had specified that only one tree out of all that He had created and given to them was off limits. Their struggle was about whether to obey God or to set their own rules; to believe that God knew what was best for them or to doubt His motives for keeping them from the tree; to walk away or to try to make themselves Godlike in having knowledge of good and evil. We all know how the story goes: They took the fruit and, in doing so, they chose their own desires over obedience to God and placed a higher value on the things that God had created than on the Creator Himself.

Those choices were the problem for Adam and Eve, and for the children of Israel, as we can read in their history recorded in the Old Testament. In fact, choosing our own way, and a lack of trust in God and obedience to His instructions continues to be the fundamental issue for us today. The problem has never been "*Will* we worship?" We were created to worship, so worship comes as naturally to us as breathing. The real question is "*Who* or *what* will we worship?" We think of idols as those weird objects carved out of wood from the Old Testament days, and we believe that we would never be so stupid as to bow down to a piece of tree. The truth is that we worship things that are equally as powerless to help us, such as money or television. How? Because making an idol out of something is simply giving it a higher priority in our lives than we give to God. Worshiping God means putting Him first and remembering that He is more important than anything or anyone else.

Covenants and Perfect Worship

In Old Testament times, a battle would end with a covenant between the victor and the vanquished that set out how they would relate to one another. But it wasn't quite the friendly chat over a cup of tea that you might think. The conqueror would set the terms of the agreement and the conquered would have to accept those terms. The way to seal the deal was not with a handshake or signing a bit of paper; they would take an animal, cut it into pieces and lay it out in two lines. As they burned the animal's body, they would walk between the pieces of smoldering flesh as a sign of the new covenant. (I'm sure that such a disgusting sight and smell would be enough to keep the memory fresh in their minds.) The conqueror set the conditions: "I'll protect you and look after you, but you will have to pay taxes to me and obey me."

When God made a covenant with Abraham and Israel, the agreement was along these lines: God said He would be their God, He would give them land to live on and a law to live by, and He would protect them from their enemies and prosper them. God could of course ask for anything He wanted in return. So what did He choose? The people were to worship and obey Him.

The fundamental step involved when we follow the command to worship God is to obey all of His other commands, because there is an act of worship and then there is an outworking of that worship in obedience. The Ten Commandments, for example, are split into two clear areas: The first four are concerned with how we relate to God, and the last six have to do with how we treat one another. The outworking of worship through obedience is a crucial idea that we need to grasp in order to fully understand what worship is. We will look at this in more detail later.

When God called Israel to be His people, He established worship to be at the heart of their life as a community, first in the tabernacle and then in the Temple. The heart of their worship was sacrifice. Up to the time of King David, whenever they came to worship, they always came with a sacrifice. There were many different types of sacrifices (Leviticus lists burnt offerings, grain offerings, fellowship offerings, sin offerings and guilt offerings). The sacrifice often involved an animal, and when it did, the significance of the act was in the shedding of the animal's blood. As it says in Leviticus 17:11, "For the life of a creature is in the blood . . . it is the blood that makes atonement for one's life." This is echoed in the New Testament: "Without the shedding of blood there is no forgiveness" (Heb. 9:22). Because life is sacred, and blood is a symbol of life, the atonement is made through the shedding of blood and the giving of a life for a life. The requirement of blood, then, points toward the ultimate sacrifice of Jesus on the cross.

These sacrifices were also tokens of creation through which the people could acknowledge that God was the One who provided them with everything they had. When at the Fall, Adam and Eve swapped their worship of the Creator for the worship of His creation, here God's people did the opposite: They put a match to God's creation in recognition of the fact that God was their first priority and worthy of all they had. With every sacrifice, they were acknowledging and repeating that God as Creator was more important than these tokens of His creation.

As we've seen, these sacrifices weren't enough to keep Israel wholeheartedly following after God. The offerings may have dented their wallets, but they didn't seem to reach in and touch their hearts. God didn't waver from His side of the bargain with Israel; it was the Israelites who didn't keep their side of the deal, choosing instead to follow other gods. As they broke the terms of the covenant, they eventually lost the land God had promised them and were sent into exile, which meant they lost the Temple—the place God inhabited, and the focus of their relationship with Him. It seemed that no human was capable of obeying the law and worshiping perfectly. They messed up again and again. This seemed to be a pattern for Israel. Throughout the Old Testament we see them coming back to God and then turning away, coming back and turning away. They couldn't worship perfectly, so God in His great mercy established a new covenant.

The basis of this new covenant was that He needed a perfect worshiper. Enter Jesus. Jesus, as representative of the human race, took upon Himself the role of keeping the law perfectly. He worshiped and obeyed His Father and thus established the new covenant, the basis of which was that God kept both sides of the deal. He was both the conqueror and the conquered; He obeyed and was obeyed. Jesus fulfilled the requirement of perfect worship through living a life of perfect worship and dying a perfect death.

Jesus lived a life of true obedience before God—a claim that not a single one of us can make no matter how holy a picture we paint of ourselves for the people around us. While Jesus' death on the cross accomplished many things—an atoning sacrifice to pay for our sins, the place where reconciliation occurred between God and humans, the place where we were freed from slavery to sin, the end of the power of death, and the place where victory over Satan was won—the heart of what Jesus did on the cross was worship. The book of Hebrews describes Jesus' death on the cross as the one perfect sacrifice. If in the Old Testament a sacrifice was given as an act of worship, then Jesus' perfect sacrifice was perfect worship. By His sacrifice, He was doing more than saying, "You, Creator God, are more important than Your creation," because Jesus was so much more than just a token of creation. He was saying, "You the Creator are more important than life itself and so I will sacrifice life itself."

The Worship Song on the Cross

As part of that perfect worship, and almost as if to underline the point, when Jesus was on the cross, He used the words from a song of worship that was written hundreds of years earlier. The words Jesus cried out on the cross are taken directly from the first line of Psalm 22: "My God, my God, why have you forsaken me?" Try reading this psalm while thinking about Jesus and the accounts of His crucifixion recorded in the New Testament. When we begin to see Psalm 22 in this light, it is clear that although David wrote this psalm, it is undeniably about Jesus. I have pulled out some key verses here to show you what I mean.

"But I am a worm and not a man, scorned by men and despised by the people. All who see me mock me; they hurl insults, shaking their heads" (Ps. 22:6-7). Compare this passage with verses about Jesus from Matthew 27: "They put a staff in his right hand and knelt in front of him and mocked him" (v. 29); "Those who passed by hurled insults at him, shaking their heads" (v. 39).

"He trusts in the Lord; let the Lord rescue him. Let him deliver him, since he delights in him" (Ps. 22:8). This verse is a direct reflection of the fact that they mocked Jesus while He was on the cross: "Come down from the cross, if you are the

Son of God!" (Matt. 27:40); "He saved others . . . but he can't save himself!" (v. 42).

"From birth I was cast upon you; from my mother's womb you have been my God" (Ps. 22:10). If anyone had the right to say these words, it was not King David, but the Son of Mary.

"My strength is dried up like a potsherd, and my tongue sticks to the roof of my mouth; you lay me in the dust of death" (Ps. 22:15). It is obvious that your tongue would stick to the roof of your mouth when your mouth is dry and you are thirsty. On the cross Jesus cried out, "I am thirsty" (John 19:28).

"A band of evil men has encircled me, they have pierced my hands and my feet" (Ps. 22:16). Of course we know that when Jesus was placed on the cross, His hands and feet were pierced with nails.

"They divide my garments among them and cast lots for my clothing" (Ps. 22:18). Compare this with "Dividing up his clothes, they cast lots to see what each would get" (Mark 15:24).

"From you comes the theme of my praise in the great assembly; before those who fear you I will pay my vows" (Ps. 22:25). This verse makes it most clear that the psalm is talking about Jesus. Why? Because in Hebrews 2:11-12, we read, "So Jesus is not ashamed to call them brothers. He says, 'I will declare your name to my brothers; in the presence of the congregation I will sing your praises.'"

"For he has not despised or disdained the suffering of the afflicted one" (Ps. 22:24). Of the prophecies of Jesus, we see in the Old Testament that this one mirrors the words that describe the Suffering Servant in Isaiah 53: "He was despised and rejected by men, a man of sorrows, and familiar with suffering" (v. 3).

The psalmist is telling us here that God did not despise the suffering of Jesus on the cross, but accepted it as pure worship.

And the best bit of this psalm? The ending. The song that began with the desperate cry "Why have you forsaken me?" ends with the words that bring hope and life to us all. Just five small words, but they're the difference between eternal life and death to us: "For he has done it" (Ps. 22:31). These words were echoed all those years later as Jesus died on the cross and declared, "It is finished" (John 19:30).

The Theological Basis for Worship

Jesus' dying on the cross is the basis of the new covenant that brought us back into relationship with God. Although Jesus offered the perfect sacrifice of worship, that doesn't mean we are no longer required to worship. Far from it.

Jesus told us that the greatest commandment is to "Love the Lord your God with all your heart and with all your soul and with all your mind and with all your strength" (Mark 12:30)—a commandment given to Moses that still holds true for us today.

A different way of expressing what Jesus said was the most important command is found in The Westminster Shorter Catechism (written way back in the seventeenth century), which begins with the question "What is the chief end of man?"—that is, What is man's reason for being? The answer? "The chief end of man is to glorify God and enjoy Him forever."

In Matthew 6:33, Jesus calls us to "seek first [God's] kingdom." I've heard it said that if you don't seek first His kingdom, then you don't seek it at all. We can't have divided hearts. There's no room for saying, "Lord, You are my God, but I just need to focus on my career right now" or "I've got a new girlfriend, so once the relationship's a bit more established, I'll put You first again." Jesus warns, "No one can serve two masters . . . you cannot serve both God and Money" (Matt. 6:24).

And isn't this true for all areas of our lives? We can't serve both our God and our career. We can't serve God but put our family before Him. We can't serve God and place a higher value on security than on Him. There's no room for more than one thing at the top of our priority list. If we put anything over and above God, we see everything through the eyes of that priority.

For example, if God asks us to be generous, and our top priority is not pleasing God but keeping money and security for ourselves, then we are not obeying God. God knows that for us to have maximum freedom and enjoyment of the life He's given us, we need to put Him first, to sift everything we do through a filter of "Does it please God's heart? Is it what He would have me do?" If the answer is not yes on both counts, then we shouldn't do it, because we are following our own ways and setting our own rules. When God is at the top of the list, the other priorities seem to fall in line with His way of thinking; but if anything else creeps in above Him, then we are breaking the first and most important command to love Him wholeheartedly.

"We Never Thought We Could Know God Like This"

Worship has always been a core value of Soul Survivor, the charity I work for that seeks to encourage and equip young people in their walk with Jesus. We spend a long time in our meetings singing songs of love and praise to God; and while that's not a definition of worship, it is an expression of worship. There is a clear biblical principle for using music and songs in times of worship. In the Old Testament, psalms were sung at the Temple. In the New Testament, we hear that they sang "psalms, hymns and spiritual songs" (Col. 3:16). And in the glimpse we are shown of heaven, there are songs sung by the elders, the angels, the living creatures and all of creation (see Rev. 4–5).

But we have confused ourselves a little by saying such things as "Now we'll have a time of worship" as someone at the front picks up a guitar and starts singing. Worship automatically gets equated with music; but this is wrong. The rest of the service—and indeed how we live—can be worship too. The singing is just a focus for the worship. There is a place for an act of worship and then there must be an outworking of that worship. We're going to be spending much of the rest of this book looking at that outworking; but first let's have a look at this act of worship through the singing of songs and what happens when we do this.

At our church, Soul Survivor Watford, we put a great emphasis on singing songs of worship in our meetings, not because we're more musically talented than others, but because when we fell in love with Jesus, singing worship songs was the first way we wanted to express that love. We wanted to tell Him how much He meant to us, to adore Him publicly and privately by singing words of love and praise, to give something back to Him for all that He had given to us. One thing we quickly discovered was that you can't out-give the Giver. As we sang to

Him, He met with us in ways we'd never expected. As we told Him we loved Him, He poured more love into our hearts. As we proclaimed how worthy He was, He began to deal with our own sense of identity and instilled in us the knowledge that we are His dearly loved sons and daughters. It seems that if you give to God, it goes against His nature not to give you something back. We found that as a congregation of worshipers, we were being changed.

This idea that God does something in us as we offer Him our hearts was demonstrated to me so clearly a few years ago during a worship time at one of our summer events. I was standing by the side of the stage while Matt Redman was leading worship when I felt someone come up and nudge me. As I turned around, a young guy pressed a knuckleduster into my hand. He gave a shy smile and walked off. He was swiftly followed by a teenager who offered me a knife, and not the kind of knife he would have needed for a few days' camping in Somerset. "Could you get rid of this for me?" he asked. Bemused, I took it from him and carried on worshiping. Then another young guy approached me and handed me a number of small foil packets that I figured contained drugs. "I don't need these anymore," he said. I put them in my pocket and wondered what else would be added to my collection by the end of the evening.

Later that night, after we'd finished the meeting, I showed Matt what I'd been given. Jokingly I took the small foil packets from my pocket and said, "We could have a good smoke with these!" Matt looked down at my hand, and when his eyes met mine again there was a look of amusement there as he said, "I'd like to see you try; they're condoms!" What a poor, sad, single

Christian youth worker I was! But the point was not my ignorance (or innocence, as I prefer to view it), but the fact that in the time leading up to those people coming up to me, no one had preached. No one had said, "God doesn't want you to physically hurt people, so please give up your weapons." No one had given an even more ambiguous call to "give up the things that are holding you back from your relationship with God—the things you know He doesn't want you to be involved in anymore." And if we'd sung the line "I will offer up my life and my condoms," then I had missed it. What we had done was worship together. During that time the Holy Spirit was able to move in people's hearts. Jesus said of the Holy Spirit, "He will convict the world of guilt in regard to sin and righteousness and judgment" (John 16:8).

Another group came one summer bringing with them a stash of drugs. They had never met with Jesus before. They just fancied a few days away from their parents and thought Soul Survivor would be a laugh. But then they came to the main meetings and got friendly with some of the Christians there. They came up to me at the end of the week and told me how they had given their lives to Jesus. With their new friends, they'd gone into a field, buried the drugs under the grass and asked their friends to pray for them as they became Christians. (I'm sure the cows in Somerset have never been quite the same.)

As a youth leader, I've had to do The Sex Talk more times than I care to remember. But what I've found is that the best way for all of us to understand where our boundaries should be is when we meet with Jesus. And it's the same when it comes to trying to give up drugs, to quit smoking or swearing, or trying to be nicer to each other. Knowing Jesus and how He lived and how He wants us to live is the best encouragement anybody can get—because it's not about the words we use; it's about knowing and loving Jesus. When we know and love Him, we can't help but want to be like Him and do what pleases Him. As Jesus said, "If anyone loves me, he will obey my teaching . . . He who does not love me will not obey my teaching" (John 14:23-24). As God meets with us and changes our hearts, we begin to realize that it's not about following a bunch of rules. It's about knowing what makes the God we love happy, and longing to please Him.

When these young people who buried their drugs told me their story, I asked them what had made them decide to follow Jesus. "Was it the humorous teaching?" I asked. "The story I told about the chocolate cake—that was a good one, wasn't it? The eloquence of the way I delivered the message? The intellectual way I opened up the Bible?"

They shook their heads more violently than I would have liked and responded, "It was the worship. We never thought we could know God like this."

True worship brings us closer to the heart of God, which is why from the time of creation He laid worship at the very foundation of our life with Him. Once we've grasped the truth that God longs for our worship before anything else, and once we understand why, we will long to give Him what He desires. What we need to know now is what that worship might look like.

CHAPTER TWO

The Worship God Requires

Over the years we have seen many worship wars in the Church. We've argued over traditional or modern, organ or guitar, louder or quieter, intimacy or celebration, this worship leader or that one. Mostly, if we're honest, the disagreements are about our preferences and prejudices. The main question we should be asking is, What kind of worship does God require? So, back to the Bible!

The easiest way to get an idea of the worship in the Old Testament is to take a look at the book of Psalms, which could be called the hymn and prayer book of Israel. Written by a number of authors, these psalms are the expression not just of King David's worship but also of all God's people at the time.

Psalms of Total Honesty

If you go back and look at the book of Psalms through the eyes of a worshiper, you might be taken aback by one distinguishing feature displayed there: complete and utter honesty. The psalmists held nothing back when expressing to God what was going on in their heads and hearts. Their words spill forth in expressions of praise, songs of victory, and proclamations of God's goodness and faithfulness. However, the striking thing is that this is all interwoven with songs of lament and exile and expressions of pain and confusion, alongside confession of sin.

Some of the psalms could almost be mistaken as the private prayer journal entries of people who suffered from extreme mood swings, soaring from the highest heights of knowing God's intimate presence and mighty power then crashing to the depths of despair at times when they felt as if they'd been abandoned and forsaken by the Almighty. To be honest, if I'd written them, I wouldn't have wanted some of the psalms to see the light of day in case people thought my faith was weak; but these no-holds-barred psalms in the Bible are included for all to see to show us what it means to have an intimate relationship with God.

It seems that God wasn't embarrassed by David and the other writers who poured out their hearts to Him. There's no sense of Him saying, "Oops, sorry about David—he was having a bad day, but it's okay; he's over it now. He was over-tired and a bit emotional, that's all. Of course I hadn't left him or forgotten him. He knows it was foolish talk, so we'll just edit those bits out to save him from embarrassment. Why don't we substitute the line where he says, 'You have put me in the lowest pit, in the darkest depths' (Ps. 88:6) with the one where he says, 'You are mighty, O Lord, and your faithfulness surrounds you' (Ps. 89:8)? After all, the high points are far more encouraging for others."

Too often we don't know how to handle people's cries to God. We worry that they're not being reverent and are therefore offending God with their questions; but the psalms make it pretty clear that God wants us to pour it all out to Him—every emotion. Jesus didn't have much time for people who were so busy putting on a show of holiness that they forgot to get their hearts right before His Father. In John 4:23-34, for example, when Jesus meets a Samaritan woman at Jacob's well, He tells her, "True worshipers will worship the Father in spirit and truth, for they are the kind of worshipers the Father seeks."

The amazing safety of our relationship with God is that we can tell Him anything and everything, and He's not surprised. We can tell Him our sin. Our fears and doubts are not hidden from Him, however much we try to bury them within ourselves. God is not like a human who will respond from a place of hurt or confusion, but He does require openness and honesty if we want to have a truly intimate relationship with Him. We belittle God when we think He can't handle our emotions and questions. The psalms, along with the book of Job in particular, illustrate that it's okay for us to question and be real about what we're going through. Honesty is what God requires. If it's going through our heads and our hearts, then let's bring it before our Father.

Sometimes I think we worry about God's reputation, as though by expressing pain we're letting Him down and making people think He's not all that He is. But God doesn't justify Himself by telling us what was going on behind the scenes and adding footnotes to the psalms. His greatness and goodness are fact, even though we have struggles in life.

Songs of Lament

A few years ago, Matt Redman and I went to see Graham Cray, who was then the principal of a vicar factory (aka theological college) in Cambridge. This man was a theological genius.

We were there on one of our regular visits to just double-check our theology and make sure we weren't inadvertently committing heresy. We chatted pleasantly until I asked him where he thought we were going wrong. I was prepared for many of the questions that could have been thrown my way, but what Graham asked was something that God had been stirring in his own heart. He said, "Where is the place of lament in our worship songs?" I wondered what he was talking about. "The songs of exile and brokenness?" he continued. "By the rivers of Babylon we sat down and wept when we remembered Zion," Graham quoted.

Thankfully, I kept my mouth shut just long enough to remember that this was written in the psalms long before Boney M turned it into a song. Still, I thought, *Poor Graham. He just doesn't get it. He's spent too much time in Bible college and can't see the theological wood for the trees.* With my most patronizing smile, I reassured him, "We're not in exile anymore, Graham. When Jesus died on the cross, He brought us home. We don't need to lament, only praise."

I sat back, waiting for him to thank me for my theological insight and then I saw the look on his face. "Who on earth told you that?" he asked. "Is this world really home? Are we not strangers in a foreign land? Yes, on the cross Jesus broke the power of sin and restored our relationship with God. Yes, the Kingdom has come now. But in another sense it is not yet in its fullness. The lion does not yet lie down with the lamb. Surely there's still a place for lament over our sin; and just because we've become Christians doesn't mean we're immune to pain in our own lives. Quite aside from us, what about the rest of the world and all the people in desperate pain and need because of war, diseases like AIDS, and natural disasters? Isn't there some room in our worship to cry out for those situations?"

In the days, weeks and months after speaking to Graham, I began to realize what we've so often missed. We've focused on the joyful bits of praise, on the happy songs that express delight at being in relationship with Jesus, exalting God for all He is and does. While this joyful praise is completely fitting and right, it only tells part of the story. It is estimated that 70 percent of the psalms are actually songs of lament rather than rejoicing. Of course we should spend much of our worship in praise and thanksgiving because God is good all the time and He is above our circumstances; we adore Him even when life hurts. Yet the psalms teach us that we can express the hurts of life, cry out to God in intercession and still adore Him. Worship was never meant to be an escape from reality. Praising His name in the midst of real pain in a real world is real worship.

The Balance Between Honesty and Truth

Worship is a place where we can bring all our pain to God; but sometimes in our desire to hold on to the truth, we have sacrificed something of our honesty. We must of course be careful to not wallow in self-indulgent pity in the name of honesty. We must look to strike a balance. The psalms incorporate honesty about where the psalmists are as well as the truth about who God is, and we must look to do the same in our worship.

One recent song that undoubtedly models the effective blending of praise and sorrow was written by Tim Hughes and is called "When the Tears Fall."

I've had questions, without answers,
I've known sorrow, I have known pain.
But there's one thing that I'll cling to,
You are faithful, Jesus, You're true.

When hope is lost, I'll call You Savior,
When pain surrounds, I'll call You healer,
When silence falls, You'll be the song within my heart.

In the lone hour of my sorrow,
Through the darkest night of my soul,
You surround me and sustain me,
My defender forever more.

I will praise You, I will praise You,
When the tears fall, still I will sing to You,
I will praise You, Jesus, praise You,
Through the suffering still I will sing.[1]

The great thing about this song is that Tim is not denying the pain that he's experiencing, and he expresses suffering while holding to the truth that God is good and faithful whether Tim feels it or not. He acknowledges that even in the "darkest night of the soul" God is right there with him in the midst of the pain, not waiting for him to get back to a happy place to come and sing a joyful song. I love the line "When hope is lost, I'll call You Savior." We still praise Him as Savior even while we mourn and grieve. To sing to God as the tears fall is true spiritual maturity; to pretend there are no tears, or worse, there *should* be no tears, is naïve.

I know that sometimes my worship feels the most meaningful when I bring my pain to Jesus. I pour out my heart, tell Him how much it hurts and then say in the midst of the pain, "I will praise You." Because in one sense, it's easy to worship God when life is going our way, when God feels close, when work and relationships are all ticking along nicely, when the sun's shining and the birds are singing. It can seem harder to worship when we're in great physical pain, grieving the loss of a loved one, confused about which direction our life is headed, when we have just had our hopes and dreams crushed or just can't seem to find God. But that's the place where we need to worship. When circumstances in our life don't seem to back it up, we need to know the truth in our heart that God is faithful, good, loving, kind and worthy of all our praise. Because of Jesus' death on the cross, we no longer have to bring physical sacrifices to God when we worship—He made the ultimate sacrifice. But there is still a place for sacrifice today and often it is here, worshiping through the tears.

David and Job are the classic biblical illustrations of worship through suffering. David was a man after God's own heart (see Acts 13:22), and we see something of what that heart is when we hear how David responded to tragedy. God took David's son's life after David's sinful relationship with Bathsheba, and when David heard that his child was dead, "he went into the house of the Lord and worshiped" (2 Sam. 12:20). Then there is Job, who was considered "blameless and upright" (Job 1:1) in the eyes of the Lord, but Satan tried to prove that Job only loved God because of what God had given him and not for who God was. This theory was blown out of the water when in just one day, Job lost his sons, daughters and livelihood and yet on hearing the news "he fell to the ground in worship" (Job 1:20).

While David and Job are two extreme examples of worshiping through the most painful of circumstances, they demonstrate hearts that were clearly in love with the Creator and not with the things He created. These men held the Giver and not the gifts in the highest esteem. Therefore, even in excruciating circumstances, they were able to praise God's name and declare the truth that He is good. This is a great reminder to us that our praise does not depend on our circumstances or how we feel. God is worthy yesterday, today and forever, and absolutely nothing can change that.

In Psalm 77, we see the writer going through one of the tough times that we all experience: "'Will the Lord reject forever? . . . Has God forgotten to be merciful?' . . . I will remember the deeds of the Lord; yes, I will remember your miracles of long ago. I will meditate on all your works and consider all your mighty deeds" (vv. 7,9,11-12). When things get hard in my life I find it easy to look at the circumstances and wonder if God has forgotten me. I start to question whether He is really involved in my life; but praising Him reminds me of His goodness. As the psalmist encourages us here, calling to mind God's faithful deeds of the past gives us hope for His faithfulness in the current trials we face. Thanksgiving fixes our eyes back on Him, brings to mind His nature and works and keeps us from too much unhelpful navel-gazing.

We have to be careful, however, that worship doesn't become a quick fix—the Christian equivalent of sinking a bottle of whiskey or taking a tablet. Our consumerist culture tells us that life revolves around our pleasure, and it's this attitude that has contributed to the way we often look at times of worship in music as something for us. We mustn't have a consumer attitude of "What can I get out of the worship? What blesses me? What gives me a quick pick-me-up?" We must remember that worship is about offering our hearts to God.

In recent years, I've heard people saying, "I can't wait for Sunday so that I can spend some time in worship. It's been such a bad week and I need some relief." It's great to long to praise God—although we don't have to wait until we meet as a church to do it—but we mustn't use it like a God-fix to see us through the week. Christianity is not about escapism. Rather than give us an hour's respite, worship should sharpen our awareness of the things going on in our lives and in the world as we bring them before the One who has power over them.

A Righteous Anger

Israel, it seems, had no problem with bringing their cries against the evil and injustice happening to them and to those around them into their songs to God. Psalm 55 tells us how David cried out to the Lord when a former friend turned against him and was leading a conspiracy against him. He said, "Let death take my enemies by surprise, let them go down alive to the grave, for evil finds lodging among them. . . . My companion attacks his friends. . . . His speech is smooth as butter, yet war is in his heart; his words are more soothing than oil, yet they are drawn swords (vv. 15,20-21).

We've often thought that anger is a sin, and that's true when we get angry about things we shouldn't. Many times in the Bible, God's anger burns because His people are not doing as He has commanded them. We too should have a righteous anger about some of the terrible situations that are going on in the world right now. Worship and intercession often go hand in hand as we allow God to break our hearts with the things that break His, and we should in turn bring the cries back to His throne room. Or, as in Psalm 55, David is expressing his anger at the betrayal of his friend. He feels it so strongly that he prays that his enemies would die; but he is quick to say, "Cast your cares on the Lord and he will sustain you" (v. 22).

Rather than keeping hold of his anger or laying into someone else, David chooses to let it out before God and then to trust that God is capable of bringing about the appropriate justice. We shouldn't use times of worship to stir up anger, but rather to pour it out to God before we turn again to face our troubled world.

Worship that acknowledges that we love God in and from a place of pain is a worship that will speak with integrity to a broken and hurting world.

The Worship of Heaven—Revelation 4-5

Ultimately, if we want to know what our worship should look like, sound like and be like, we would do well to catch a glimpse of the worship in heaven. In Revelation, chapters 4 and 5, God, through the apostle John, gives us such a glimpse. Let us look at these verses section by section and see what they show us.

At once I was in the Spirit, and there before me was a throne in heaven with someone sitting on it. And the one who sat there had the appearance of jasper and carnelian. A rainbow, resembling an emerald, encircled the throne (4:2-3).

The first thing we see is a throne with someone sitting on it. I'm sure that a great theologian could tell you the symbolic significance of the jasper and carnelian, but my intellectual assessment would be that they are very colorful. I know, my insight is astounding at times. But anyway, add to that an emerald rainbow and we're starting to build a very vibrant picture.

Surrounding the throne were twenty-four other thrones, and seated on them were twenty-four elders. They were dressed in white and had crowns of gold on their heads (4:4).

You may not be able to imagine it if you've seen the suave and sophisticated way I dress, but believe it or not I owe my dashing dress sense to some wise words from friends. You see, I used to have a habit of not really looking at what I was putting on in the morning. I'd get up, find any pair of trousers that were clean, pick one of my fantastically colorful shirts and that would be pretty much all the thought that went into my dressing routine. One morning when I was out in California with my friends Matt and Beth, I knew I was in trouble because Beth sent Matt over to talk to me. The thing is, I had put on one of my favorite shirts with a pair of Bermuda shorts that were equally brightly patterned. The words delivered were gentle but made a significant point. "Mike," Matt said, "when you're thinking about what to wear, why don't you try and remember a little rule of Beth's? If you want to wear a snazzy top, then wear it with plain trousers. If you want to wear a pair of trousers that have a pattern, then wear them with a simple top. To be honest, if you wanted to just wear a plain top and plain trousers, that would be fine too. But please, for all our sakes, don't wear a snazzy top with snazzy trousers!"

I've taken these words to heart. So when I looked in Revelation, I was pleased to see that the 24 elders seemed to be on the same wavelength as Beth when it came to dressing. They wore plain white robes, which meant all the attention could be focused on their magnificent, brightly shining gold crowns.

> From the throne came flashes of lightning, rumblings and peals of thunder. Before the throne, seven lamps were blazing. These are the seven spirits of God. Also before the throne there was what looked like a sea of glass, clear as crystal (4:5-6).

In addition to color, we now get the light and sound show, and I would hazard a guess that this was *loud*; after all, we *are* talking thunder! And the lights are not just pretty candles flickering or fairy lights twinkling; these are blazing with huge flames that add to the color and majesty of the picture. And all of these things are reflected in the mirror of the sea of glass, just to make sure there's an extra wow factor. What does this tell us? That if there's one thing we'd better not forget to pack when we go to heaven, it's our sunglasses!

John goes on to describe the uniqueness of the four living creatures: one like a lion, the second like an ox, another like a man, and the other like an eagle. And then we get to the song:

> Day and night they never stop saying: "Holy, holy, holy is the Lord God Almighty, who was, and is, and is to come" (4:8).

Do you realize that this phrase is constantly and forever being repeated? All the time. No break. No change in wording. They gave the chorus a few minutes ago and by the time you finish reading this line they'll be doing it all over again. And of course it doesn't end there.

> Whenever the living creatures give glory, honor and thanks to him who sits on the throne and who lives forever and ever, the twenty-four elders fall down before him who sits on the throne, and worship him who lives forever and ever. They lay their crowns before the throne and say: "You are worthy, our Lord and God, to receive glory and honor and power, for you created all things, and by your will they were created and have their being" (4:9-11).

Every time the four living creatures have finished doing their "holy, holy, holy" bit, they step back and the 24 old guys take their turn. They get off their thrones, fall down on their faces, cast their crowns in front of the big throne and deliver their words of praise.

Then, when they've done that, the four living creatures repeat their "holy, holy, holy" lines, during which the elders put their crowns back on and get back on the thrones so they are ready to jump off and throw down their crowns again on cue. The same thing gets repeated over and over and over again. I'm sure it's not the only thing that disqualifies me, but I know I'm nowhere near fit enough to be one of the 24 elders.

Then I looked and heard the voice of many angels, numbering thousands upon thousands, and ten thousand times ten thousand. They encircled the throne and the living creatures and the elders. In a loud voice they sang: "Worthy is the Lamb, who was slain, to receive power and wealth and wisdom and strength and honor and glory and praise!" (5:11-12).

So what about us? Where do we come in?

Then I heard every creature in heaven and on earth and under the earth and on the sea, and all that is in them, singing: "To him who sits on the throne and to the Lamb be praise and honor and glory and power, for ever and ever!" (5:13).

We're the creatures on Earth and we join in with the animals of the air, the earth and the sea to sing God's praise. Then, and I love this:

The four living creatures said, "Amen!" (5:14).

After all the color and light and noise of what we've just seen, this is something of an anticlimax! But it's all it takes to set off those Duracell-powered elders, and they fall down and worship again.

The Heart of Worship

What a picture! How breathtaking and awe-inspiring is the worship of heaven—full of color and creativity, sound and light, praise and adoration! But if we leave it there, we miss something—and not just a little something either. Right in the middle, we read that there was a scroll with seven seals, and an angel who proclaimed in a loud voice:

> "Who is worthy to break the seals and open the scroll?" But no one in heaven or on earth or under the earth could open the scroll or even look inside it. I wept and wept because no one was found who was worthy to open the scroll or look inside. Then one of the elders said to me, "Do not weep! See, the Lion of the tribe of Judah, the Root of David, has triumphed" (5:2-5).

You see, all of the other stuff we've been looking at is just the warm-up act—merely a sideshow to the main event. While the crowns are being thrown and the lightning is flashing, John introduces us to the star of the show, the One we've been waiting for. The thunder rumbles as the curtains open and all the creatures in heaven and on Earth let out a gasp at what they see: a lamb.

Then I saw a Lamb, looking as if it had been slain, standing in the center of the throne, encircled by the four living creatures and the elders (5:6).

This is Jesus. All the loud noise, fireworks, clapping and cheering and jumping around, all of it is for the One who is the Lion of the tribe of Judah. And this mighty Lion, this all-conquering Savior, appears as a lamb that's been slain. Just as God's people often used lambs as offerings of worship to atone for their sin, God Himself provides His only Son as the sacrificial Lamb that defeats sin forever. He is at the center of it all.

If Jesus is at the center of the worship of heaven, He must be at the center of the worship on Earth. So you see, it's really not about who leads worship, whether the lights are bright and flashing or turned down low, whether the lead guitarist has been playing for 10 years or 10 days, or whether you stand near the front or the back of church. We may never have seven blazing lamps or a sea of crystal-clear glass, and we may have more than 24 old guys trying to get in on the act, but it's not about that. It's about Jesus, because He is so magnificent. He is awesome and wonderful, the King of kings and Lord of lords, but He will appear to us as a lamb that was slain because the King of the universe, through whom all things were created, shed His blood on a wooden cross and died for us. And that should always be at the heart of our worship.

Because He is amazing, we give ourselves in worship not just in words and song, but also in our hearts. When we come before

Him, we realize afresh that we should hold nothing back. He is worthy of it all. Even offering up our lives seems like nothing in comparison to His glory. Our worship must go far beyond the music; it must infuse every area of our lives.

CHAPTER THREE

Worship as a Lifestyle

Society has been telling us for years that the way to contentment is having all of our desires fulfilled as quickly as possible. We're bombarded with messages about how to make our lives more comfortable, and the messages all revolve around having our every whim realized. Strangely, no one seems to be getting any happier; they just spend more time chasing the things they want—or think they want.

To be honest, even for those of us who try to live against this culture, our natural default setting seems to be that we think the world revolves, or at the very least *should* revolve, around us. We get caught up in our decisions, our problems, our pains, our hopes and our dreams, when really it's not about us at all. Our prayers become insular and demanding. Why hasn't God given me a girlfriend? Why didn't my exams go as well as I'd hoped? What about my dreams, my desires, my heart? Me, me, me.

But when we worship, our focus shifts: When we put Jesus at the center of our lives in the knowledge of all that was given for us, we humbly remember that it's all about Him. When we fully catch this glimpse of His worth, we offer our lives gladly. But what does that look like?

Worship leader David Ruis, in his book *The Worship God Is Seeking*, wrote, "The only true expression of worship is through the abandonment of all our agendas for His, as we trust in His sovereign power and unlimited grace."[1] Worship, it seems, is about surrendering all areas of our life to God, giving Him our hearts, our careers, our money, our time and everything else at our disposal to serve Him; in all areas of life, we choose to echo Jesus' words before He went to the cross: "Not my will, but Yours be done"(Luke 22:42). These may be some of the hardest words to pray as we bring our hopes, dreams and fears to God. It costs to abandon our own agendas in favor of His, but there is no safer or more rewarding place to be.

The Offering of Our Lives

Somehow over the years we've created a hierarchy of holiness within the Church when it comes to employment. At the very top, with the ultimate way to love and serve God, are the worship leaders and big-stage evangelists. Following hot on their heels for the second seat at the table of holiness are the overseas missionaries. And of course, God clearly uses those who work full-time for the Church, so they happily slide into third place. At number four are the "worthy secular jobs"—we're talking about doctors, nurses, teachers and generally those who get paid to help others. Languishing at the bottom of the table, not valued by us and, we suppose, by God, are those of us who do "normal jobs." If you're a plumber, a secretary, an accountant or a builder, how can God possibly use you in your work? Of course the money you earn is brought back into the Church, so that's of some value, but the way you get it? Who cares?

Let me tell you about a poor fool who thought this same way. He became a Christian at the age of 16, and with a heart desperate to serve God and a passion to preach His Word, he decided that no other job would be good enough than to work full-time within the Church. His name? Mike Pilavachi. It makes me cringe to think about it now, but I became an accountant to pass the time until the call to Africa came or the worldwide Mike Pilavachi preaching road show took off. I spent the next 12 years—12 years!—asking God to rescue me. I yearned so much for Him to use me and yet missed opportunities daily for Him to do just that. I was so focused on what was in the future that I couldn't see what was right in front of me. It dawned on me slowly, and I do mean slowly, that God wanted me to be satisfied serving Him in my job whatever I was doing—that to Him, worship and service meant to go where He called me and to do the things in front of me well and to His glory.

As Paul wrote to the Colossians, "Whatever you do, work at it with all your heart, as working for the Lord, not for men, since you know that you will receive an inheritance from the Lord as a reward. It is the Lord Christ you are serving" (Col. 3:23-24). The irony is that it was only as I began to see the truth that being a full-time Christian worker simply meant doing my work with a heart of thankfulness and worship to God, and I began to appreciate the opportunities I'd been given where I was, that He opened the door to something else.

Although I regret the way I handled my time as an accountant, I'm so thankful to God for teaching me such a valuable lesson. If He'd moved me on any sooner, I would have thought that those years before I started my ministry were wasted.

"Ministry" is a much misused word in the Church today— being an accountant was as much my ministry as working as a youth leader. In God's eyes, there is no hierarchy; He doesn't find one gift more useful than another. You don't serve Him more by leading worship at church than by pouring tea and coffee in a café, or by speaking to a congregation of hundreds than by chatting to the person at the desk next to you. Everything we do, if offered to our heavenly Father and done in love, is an act of worship.

The Division of Sacred and Secular

We need to reclaim the truth that nothing is secular and everything is sacred for the Christian who wants to truly worship God with his or her life. The Hebrews' culture wasn't divided between the sacred and the secular, as we divide it. This is clear when you read the law of Moses; there's stuff about what to do in the Temple, and then on the next page there are instructions about how to handle your cattle, how to treat your wife and neighbors, and what to do with your money and your tithe. It's all in there together and we've lost how intensely practical the Bible is and how God is interested in and involved in all aspects of our lives.

One of the most inspirational books I've ever read was written by a seventeenth-century French monk called Brother Lawrence. Desperate to live in constant communion with God, he chose to become a monk and learned to practice the presence of God no matter what he was doing. The many hours he spent in the kitchen washing dishes were not wasted in his eyes, but "having taken as the end of all his actions, to do them all for the love of God, he was satisfied therewith."[2] He learned that we can invite God's presence into all areas of our lives, that true happiness comes from doing all things as an act of worship to Him, making everything we do about Him.

Because these opportunities to worship are disguised as normal parts of everyday life, they are easy to miss. A few years ago, Tim Hughes and I were in Port Elizabeth, South Africa, where we were invited to go to a Christian radio station and talk about worship. We enjoyed chatting with the host about many different aspects of worship, and the novelty of acting like experts. As we left the building and were about to get into our car, two small children came up to us. They wore ragged clothes and their faces were dirty; it was obvious they were two of the many street children in that area. They came over and begged us for some money. I patted my pockets and apologized: "I'm sorry; I don't have any change. I don't have anything to give you." We climbed into our car and watched them walk away empty-handed.

Two seconds later it hit me like a ton of bricks what had just happened: God, having just given me an opportunity to talk about worship, had also given me an opportunity to express an act of worship, and I'd totally missed it. My heart pounded until we stopped at some lights and saw the children again. Beckoning them over, I pulled out a 50-rand note (about U.S. $6) and pressed it into their hands. Their faces lit up immediately, as though I had handed them a fortune.

"Do you know where this comes from?" I asked them. "Yes, sir," they replied immediately, "from Jesus." There was no prompting, and I guess they knew the truth that I myself wasn't quick enough to see. Thankfully Jesus was living in me and He was the One who prompted me to hand over the money.

They ran off jumping for joy and I thanked God that He had given me a second chance to literally put my money where my mouth was. Giving to those boys was an act of love from me to my Savior.

From the Pews to the People Outside the Church

If we want better worship on a Sunday, then the answer probably doesn't lie in changing the order of the songs or getting a new guitarist. After we gather at church and worship with our words and our voices, we should be spending the rest of the week acting out that worship in all sorts of ways, from how we love and care for our friends and families to what we do with our money, how we carry out our work tasks and how we treat those with less than we have. If our lives don't match up to our songs, the words become meaningless; but when they do match, our praises in church are richer as they come from the overflow of hearts that have spent the entire week praising God. The music is an act of worship, but for this worship to be genuine it has to be connected to and demonstrated throughout all areas of our lives.

As we do this, we find that the happiness and satisfaction that the world tells us we can achieve through owning the coolest clothes, going on better holidays or seeing our every dream come true is not real. We can't even achieve these things, as some of us in the Church have believed, through serving the Lord by becoming a worship leader or a missionary. We can achieve happiness and satisfaction in looking for ways every day to love and bless

God, however simple those acts might be, however overlooked by others, and all the while realizing that God not only sees but accepts each as an act of devotion.

For us to respond to people and their needs as Jesus would, we need God to change our hearts to make them more like His. Amazing things happen when we worship. As we spend more time with Jesus, we begin to care about the things He cares about. Richard Foster sums it up so simply when he says in his book *Celebration of Discipline*, "To worship is to change."[3]

I'd say it was impossible to connect with God as we do in intimate times of worship and to leave unchanged. Our hearts get stretched and challenged, and we begin to long to take all that we've found in Him out onto the streets, away from the safety of the Church and to a world that needs to know its Savior. The more we see of Him, the more we want others to know about Him; it's a natural reaction when you fall in love— you want to tell people about the wonderful person you have given your heart to. It should be this infectious enthusiasm, this burning love for Jesus and sharing in His heart for the world that propels us from the pews to the people outside of the Church.

PART 2

Evangelism

Why Evangelize?

In recent years, people have written off God and the Church as irrelevant and boring—outdated and bearing no relation to their lives. We in the Church have been very good at telling people what we're against—to the point that they often have no idea what being a Christian means beyond not smoking, drinking, swearing or having sex before marriage. We've signed petitions and pointed our fingers at lifestyles we don't approve of and in so doing we've made enemies of the people who don't live life the way we do. Of course it's vitally important that we stand up for righteousness and don't water down biblical truths to fit in with society, but we seem to have so poorly represented Jesus that most people couldn't tell you what He is *for*.

If we want to better represent Jesus, then we'd be wise to remember some of His characteristics. From the Bible, but also from our own lives, we know that Jesus is loving, compassionate, full of grace and mercy, kind, humble, forgiving and passionate. Would people outside of the Church say the same about us?

A few years ago, I visited a church in North America where there was a notice displayed asking people not to use the gas station next door. Curiosity getting the better of me, I asked why, intrigued at what would stop everyone from using the facility. I was shocked by the answer. "It's run by Muslims," came the response, as though that was a reason in itself. Nothing has spoken to me more gravely of the way we have built up a "them versus us" idea, with us in the safety of the Church and them as the big bad world outside.

How on earth do we expect people to get to know the living God if we, as God's representatives on Earth, behave like that? How we treat others reflects how we think God feels about them; so what does it tell them when we boycott their business and try to ruin their livelihood? Shouldn't we be doing the opposite? Rather than being a destructive influence in someone's life because we don't agree with their beliefs, we should be blessing them and supporting them. What would have happened if that church had decided to get involved with the people running that gas station? What would have happened if they had committed to praying for them? Chosen to get involved and to love and bless them rather than showing them a cold shoulder? What would speak more of the love and compassion of Jesus?

What's the Best Way to Tell People About Jesus?

"Evangelism" has become a word that for many of us is loaded with guilt and confusion. It seems as if the Church has always known that it needs to tell the rest of the world about Jesus, but we've never been quite sure of how to go about doing it. So we've come up with strategies, theories and templates in the hope of drawing people into the Church. Sadly, these projects of ours have left many of us floundering.

Few Christians would doubt Jesus' intention when He left us with the Great Commission to "go and make disciples of all nations" (Matt. 28:19), but many would argue over the best way to go about it. Each group, having taken a good, long look at how Jesus did things in the Bible, has put its own spin on things.

For some of us it's been "proclamation evangelism." Those of us who fall into this camp believe that the best way to communicate Jesus is through direct words. We can take the words of Mark 16 to "preach the good news" as a literal translation of "preach," which means "to speak earnestly," and we can then follow the logic that Jesus preached publicly and that many people were saved. So evangelism must be about the words.

Others of us would say that it's not so much about what we say as it is about the way we live our lives. There is a world around us full of broken and hurting people. Human beings made in God's image live every day without even the basics of food and shelter, so there are plenty of needs we can meet in the name of Jesus. Those of us who believe that this is the best method of evangelism use the words of St. Francis of Assisi, who famously said, "Preach the gospel at all times and when necessary use words." This is certainly in line with the fact that when we look at Jesus, we see that it was often the things He did as well as the things He said that captured people's attention and brought them to faith. So maybe "works" is the way forward.

But there has also been yet another school of thought that it was the signs and wonders Jesus did that really opened people's hearts to the gospel. And we do see in the Gospels and the book of Acts how the blind received their sight, the sick were healed and the dead were raised to life. As a result of these things, many people put their faith in Jesus.

So which method is right? Well, these methods of evangelism are all rooted in Scripture and our understanding of how Jesus lived His life, so I would suggest that they are *all* right. The best way to communicate Jesus is with all the tools at our disposal: words, works *and* wonders. If people see Jesus in our actions but don't hear Him in our words, then how will they know their own need for a Savior or understand what it means to be in relationship with Him? And surely we're shooting ourselves in the foot if we tell people about Jesus but don't put His words into action in our own lives. On top of this there's a hunger and passion for the supernatural inside us—part of the deep call in our spirits to know that there is more to life than what we can hear, see, touch, smell and taste. When people see miracles and healings, they see something of the power of God that is hard to argue with.

Throughout His ministry, Jesus set out plain truths in His preaching, cared for the poor and the marginalized, cast out demons and healed the sick. If we use Jesus as our model for effective evangelism, then we can't deny the power to reach people using all three elements together. But even when we see that, evangelism still seems like a scary concept. If someone mentions the word "evangelism," we start to look guilty because we don't know where to begin, or we look back at times we've got ourselves all excited about evangelism and then the mission we poured our hearts into yielded little results.

Sometimes we decide that the only place we're safe from the contamination of the world is behind walls. We've tried to make the Church like a safe castle where we live apart from the rest of the world so that they can't get us. Every now and then we feel guilty because we know that Jesus called us to make disciples of all nations. So we "do a mission." We practice our Christian plays and testimonies, let down the drawbridge, run out of the castle, "do some evangelism" and hope to take some captives (by force, if necessary) to bring back with us. If by any chance we do get someone to follow us back, we do something to them that we've called "discipleship," which really seems to involve making them clones of us so that they too can't relate to anyone outside of the safety of the Church. We've called this process evangelism, but really it's anti-evangelism. We're not called to live apart from the world and only come out once or twice a year; we're called to live without walls, to be an active part of our community and to influence it for Jesus.

One of the saddest things I've seen regarding our influence for Jesus as Christians was a lesson given to a particular group of young people at a Christian conference. Many of the students in the group had just given their lives to God. These people were passionate for Jesus; they'd met Him and fallen in love and were in the process of working out how to live their lives for Him. How amazing to see God transforming people's lives! The thing that broke my heart was what they were then taught. The preacher got a young lad from the crowd and got him to stand on a chair in front of everyone. "Try and pull me up," she said, offering him her hand. He gave it his best shot, but for little reward; there was no moving her from the ground. "Now let me see if I can pull you down," she continued, and with one tug that was it—he fell from the chair. I was horrified by the point she was making—that as a Christian you can't influence others to get to know Jesus, but they will pull you away from Him. I couldn't believe that these young people were being told that if they wanted to live holy lives they needed to stop seeing their friends who didn't know Jesus.

We've so often believed that if we keep hanging out with people outside of the Church, we will be contaminated and polluted by the world. But that's the extreme opposite of the example Jesus set for us—He hung out with the worst of sinners. And it wasn't by accident or because there was no one else to talk to. He actively sought out the people who were considered the farthest from God (the thieves, the prostitutes, the drunks) and chose to spend time with them. In fact He spent so much time with them that people accused Him of being a drunkard and a glutton like them.

A biblical example that, unfortunately, most of us can relate to is that of the Pharisees. The Pharisees had built their lives on following the Word of God and keeping themselves pure and holy as He intended them to be. There were many laws about keeping oneself ceremonially clean that they followed strictly. In their desire to stay clean, they began to take things much further than God required, to the point where they would have been offended to see Jesus hang out with those they considered unholy. In this and in many other ways, Jesus came to show that the compassion of God stretched far beyond a list of rules. He didn't seem to care in the slightest about being friends with those who weren't acceptable in "polite society." He wasn't bothered about His reputation, because that wasn't His identity or His motivation, and He knew that the people He was reaching would otherwise go unnoticed by the religious leaders.

Can we say the same? Can we say that we are happy to hang out with the people society would tell us are the lowest and the least—those who will never be a part of the "in crowd"? If people judge and misunderstand us, will we be okay with that and know that no one has a higher or lower place in God's eyes?

So, if Jesus wasn't interested in building up a good reputation for Himself, what was His motivation for hanging out with sinners? This is a key point for us, because our motivation needs to be the same. We'll look at that in more detail in the next chapter.

For now, we can say that we can't win brownie points with God to try to get what we want in return or to try to earn His love. Neither can we be motivated by guilt or pressure from those around us. Jesus knew what being in relationship with His Father could do for people; He knew the joy and blessing of having a friendship with the Father, and He wanted us to share in that. He also knew that God is worthy of every person's love and life, and He wanted His Father to have the praise and glory that are rightfully His.

At the heart of all this is the key defining factor: love. God did not open a window in heaven and shout, "I love you." He sent His Son to live side by side with us. And we need to do the same. Loving people from a distance doesn't work anywhere near as well as getting to know them and being a part of their lives. The bottom line is that Jesus was motivated by compassion and love for His Father's creation.

CHAPTER FIVE

Jesus' Strategy

A few years ago, a friend of mine sat me down and shattered any remaining illusions I had that I was still young. "Mike," he said, with a comforting pat on the shoulder, "you're not as young as you used to be. You need to start conserving your energy." While I tried to plaster a convincing smile on my face and gather the remaining shreds of my ego, he continued, "You don't seem to have a strategy for what meetings you speak at. Where you go and whom you see is all disconnected. Shouldn't you be a bit more strategic and start saying no to engagements where there are fewer than 500 people? What you need to focus your time and energy on are the people with power and influence. Go and speak to the leaders and shapers of this generation, because they are the people you need to catch if you want to have the widest impact."

For a few minutes, that advice made sense to me. Maybe I had been a bit haphazard in where I went. Maybe I needed to think a bit more about the people I was reaching. After all, I wanted as many people as possible to know about Jesus. But then it got me thinking: Why didn't anyone tell Jesus to be more strategic in targeting the people He hung around with? Poor Jesus! Take the disciples as an example: what a strange lot they were, and yet He *chose* them all to be His closest friends. This group was made up of a bunch of fishermen (two guys with short tempers—James and John—earned their nickname "Sons of Thunder"); a tax collector; a zealot (who was revolutionary);

and Judas to top it all off. Forgive me for saying it, but they were hardly the "in crowd."

Jesus obviously hadn't heard the latest theories on catching the leaders. He just went to any old person, with little consideration of their power and status. And, if we're honest, the people to whom He gave priority and went to first were all the *wrong* people. Hardly a leader or influential celebrity among them—in fact, they were more like the anti-movers and shakers, the lowest of the low. Some of the people He chose to hang out with were the kind of people no one noticed except perhaps to scorn and avoid. Yes, Jesus did eventually take on the powers at Jerusalem, but He did that much later, after He'd spent time with the others.

In the Church, we've always wanted a crowd; we've wondered how to draw the maximum number of people into our services and festivals, mistaking numbers as a sign that what we're doing has the power and authority of heaven. But it doesn't sound as if Jesus had a problem attracting a crowd—there's no record at the Sermon on the Mount of His disciples counting the crowd and asking Jesus if there were enough people for Him to bother with, or if He'd like to postpone till they could get more people. He didn't say, "I'm not doing a miracle for just 5,000. Get me a crowd of 50,000 and I'll show you how to have a feast with a few loaves and fishes." Whereas we're obsessed with trying to build a crowd, Jesus was usually trying to escape one. So many times we read that a crowd had gathered and, rather than getting excited, Jesus got into a boat and rowed off or went up a mountain to pray all night alone. He did not seem to care about the strategies my friend was telling me to employ.

When Jesus passed through Jericho, for example, He didn't seek out the person we might have expected in order to unlock the hearts and minds of the rest of the town for Him. We would probably have picked someone with power and influence—but not Jesus. He knew that the guy He needed to speak to was the short bloke who had climbed halfway up a tree to observe Jesus and the crowd around Him. "Hey, Zac! I have to come to your house tonight," Jesus called to him. If you picture the scene, you can imagine the stir this caused. The Bible even highlights how unpopular a move this was when the people grumbled, "Doesn't He know Zacchaeus is the chief tax collector?" In those days a tax collector was not a civil servant, as we know them today (although some would say this would have been reason enough to avoid him). His job actually made him a traitor to Israel. Zacchaeus spent his days collecting on behalf of the occupying Roman authority and stealing from his own people, making himself very rich in the process. He would have been despised, a social outcast, and yet he was the one Jesus picked out to have dinner with.

On another note, I have to say that for a number of years the parable of the lost sheep in Luke 15 caused me some confusion. I thought that when the shepherd left the 99 to go in search of the one missing sheep, he would have paid due care and attention and locked up the 99 in a safe and secure pen with at least two other shepherds on duty to look after them while he went off. I don't pretend to know much about shepherding, but that would have made sense to me. But if that were the case, there would be no point to the story. No, this particular shepherd left the 99 sheep still in his possession on the side of a hill where they were bound to wander off and get lost. So when Jesus told this story, everyone listening would have thought, "What a weird shepherd. He's rejoicing because he found the one sheep that he lost, but he must be *really* stupid not to realize that he lost 99 to do it." Then Jesus hits them with the punch line: God is like that shepherd.

The point of the story, which I had so often missed, is not that God doesn't protect His own but that He sees individuals. He wants to be involved, to have us comprehend the intimate care with which He watches over us. Each individual person matters to Him—that's the main point of the parable. Thus, Jesus had a strategy, but it wasn't motivated by a need to speak to big crowds or to get His message as far and wide as possible. His strategy was to love. He cared for and had compassion on individuals. Now that's a strategy worth making our own.

Of course we pray and long for lots of people to know Jesus; but rather than seeing a mass of people waiting to be converted, we need to see with Jesus' eyes—to see people one at a time and to see each person's particular needs.

Many times we read in the Gospels that Jesus had compassion on people, but we don't always fully take in what that meant. The Greek word Jesus used for "compassion" literally meant "a tearing of the gut." One time when Jesus used this word was the time when He met a man who had leprosy, which we can read about in Mark 1:40-45. It is likely this man was not only suffering from his physical ailments but from the emotional pain of being cast out from society as well. People with leprosy in those days were forced to announce their presence everywhere they went to allow others time to get away from them. But this man dared to come close to Jesus, kneel before Him and make his request to be made clean. Jesus didn't recoil in horror, as anyone else around Him would have done. Instead, "Filled with compassion, Jesus reached out his hand and touched the man. 'I am willing,' he said. 'Be clean!'" (Mark 1:41).

What I love about this is that Jesus not only healed the man's physical condition, but He must have restored so much more in the man's heart. Jesus probably would have been the first person to touch this man in years, and He did it from a place of love and desire for the man to be whole.

Jesus' concern was often very practical too. The feeding of the 4,000, for example, took place after He said, "I have compassion for these people; they have already been with me three days and have nothing to eat" (Mark 8:2).

Of course, spiritual need touched Jesus deeply. *THE MESSAGE* tells us that when Jesus saw a crowd, "his heart broke—like sheep with no shepherd they were. He went right to work teaching them" (Mark 6:34). Jesus never patronized or looked down on people. He responded to them from a place of genuine compassion and love.

Loving Sinners

We live in a world full of lonely and hurting people. This is an age when hope often seems hard to come by and where one of our favorite phrases is "You don't get something for nothing." In the face of this mind-set, we need to meet people's needs, to get to know them, to love them, to see them just as Jesus saw Zacchaeus and the man with leprosy. We need to care for individuals not because we want to rack up the numbers of people on our evangelism quota but because we love them. We need to share God's heart for people so that like Jesus we're not looking down on people but are caring for them.

Whereas Jesus hated the sin and loved the sinner, we seem to have gotten ourselves confused. For example, I think that one of the things that must break Jesus' heart is the fact that the last place someone who is homosexual feels that he or she can feel accepted and loved is with the Church. We've brought a message of judgment and condemnation rather than the message of hope and love Jesus brings. One of our favorite verses is John 3:16: "For God so loved the world that he gave his one and only Son, that whoever believes in him shall not perish but have eternal life." Understandably, it brings us great joy that we are both loved and saved, but we mustn't see this as a message only for those of us who already believe. The next verse says, "For God did not send his Son into the world to condemn the world, but to save the world through him."

No wonder "the tax collectors and 'sinners' were all gathering around to hear him" (Luke 15:1). What a message of hope! Jesus didn't come to condemn us, to point the finger and go through a whole list of our sins, but to save the world He loves. When we look at those outside of the Church, we must remember that God loves them just as much as He loves us and that we too are sinners. The difference is that our sins have been paid for through the blood of Jesus, and we have accepted—not earned—God's love for us.

A few years ago, I went on a trip to Australia with some friends. We met a guy called Ben, who took us to his church, which turned out to be in the red-light district of Melbourne. To me it seemed an odd place to have a church, but Ben explained how God had been breaking his heart for the people that no one in the Church was reaching out to and caring for, and how he joined this church that ministered to both past and present drug addicts and to people who are gay. They didn't minister from a distance; many of the church members, including those with young families, moved from the safety and comfort of the suburbs to live right there in the red-light district to love the people they came into contact with.

They weren't a church that watered down God's commandments or hid from the truths that the Bible makes clear. But what they shouted loudest was that God loves. Rather than throwing stones, they modeled holy lifestyles. They chose to celebrate marriage with excitement and enthusiasm rather than teach on its virtues in order to condemn those who didn't conform.

It is no surprise that they've seen lots of people come to Jesus in that church. Society had given up on many of these people: drug addicts who for years had barely been able to think about anything except their next fix, and teenagers so broken and despairing that suicide attempts had become a regular event. Ben and the members of his congregation didn't point out these people's mistakes or criticize their lifestyle choices; instead they pointed to the love and acceptance of Jesus.

They called their church "Matthew's Party" after the disciple who was a tax collector when Jesus called him. When Matthew threw a party for Jesus, the only people he knew to invite were people like himself: the other outcasts, sinners and drunks. What an amazing name for a church! It sums up all that they are about—not an exclusive "members only" club, but the kind of place where everyone is welcome.

We all remember the story from John 8 known as "the story of the woman caught in adultery." Or at least that's how we think of it. Shouldn't it really be "Jesus and the men caught holding stones"? The woman walked away forgiven by Jesus. The men were the ones whose sin had been uncovered, their hard hearts wanting to judge and condemn her for her actions.

It wasn't that Jesus was too soft on people, but He knew that the most powerful way to bring about change in a person's life was to love them. Don't we all know that from our own lives? Generally the people who have shaped and molded us, from whom we've learned the most, are the people who have invested time and energy in getting to know us, people we can relax and have a laugh with and, most important, who love us. But the sad truth is that throughout the centuries, we, the Body of Christ, often have been so busy throwing stones that we've forgotten that we need to put them down and love people first.

The people who go to Matthew's Party are loved unconditionally, and they belong with the people of that congregation whether they choose to accept Jesus or not. They don't have to get all cleaned up and comply with any standards; they are welcomed into the church with open arms, just as Jesus welcomed people.

Belong, Believe and Behave

Traditionally we've told people they are welcome to join us at church, but they have to fit in with us and behave as we do: stand when we stand, sit when we sit and no kissing in the back row— that kind of thing. If they manage to stay long enough to hear and respond to the gospel, then they can believe in Jesus and, at that point, we baptize them, which is when we say they belong and are part of the Church family.

Jesus, on the other hand, showed us a very different way. When He chose His disciples, He called them to follow Him way before their behavior changed (take James and John arguing over who was the most important; all of them falling asleep in Gethsemane when Jesus had asked them to pray; Peter lying when Jesus was arrested and saying he'd never known Him). They didn't even understand who Jesus was for a long time; but right from the start, Jesus let them know that they belonged with Him, believing and behaving, or not. The truth is, we don't really see their behavior changing until we get to the book of Acts.

We also see this "belong first, believe second, behave third" attitude in many of Jesus' other relationships. He didn't say to Zacchaeus, "Stop your stealing, then I'll think about talking to you." No. Jesus said, "I want to eat with you, Zacchaeus, to be friends. Let's hang out." And because He did that, because He loved Zacchaeus as he was, Zacchaeus changed. From the overflow of Zacchaeus's heart, he didn't grumble that he had to give back all he'd stolen from his countrymen. He gave it all back willingly and then some. He added to his repentance by giving away half of all his possessions. As far as we know, Jesus hadn't even said a word about what was wrong in Zac's life. I think it just became glaringly obvious to him when Jesus picked him out of the crowd and loved him.

Jesus didn't wait for people to clean themselves up before He loved them, and neither should we. It's a sobering thought to imagine where you or I would be if Jesus had demanded holiness before He forgave us and welcomed us into new life. But the truth is that "while we were still sinners, Christ died for us" (Rom. 5:8).

CHAPTER SIX

From Water to Worship

When I was at university, I was very proud of being given the label "God Squad" by my fellow students. I thought it meant that I was doing a fantastic job of preaching about Jesus, whereas I think I was just putting people off. I had a strategy that I would employ every lunchtime, using a booklet based on the Four Spiritual Laws as my weapon of choice. The booklet itself was actually a great resource, but my use of it could be considered more of an abuse.

I would stake out the campus canteen and look for a poor, unsuspecting person to be my victim. I had a finely tuned sense, like a lion that spots a buffalo straying from the safety of the herd and knows exactly when to pounce. As I sat down opposite this unfortunate person, I would grin from ear to ear and wait. The person would look up and see my grin. He or she would look down and I'd still be grinning. Sure enough he'd look up again, wondering why I hadn't gone away, and still I would smile until the person was completely unnerved. Then I'd introduce myself and ask the person's name and then say, "Good to meet you, [insert name of random stranger]. Have you thought about your eternal destiny?" During the next few moments, when the person looked both confused and somewhat frightened, I would wade in with diagrams and illustrations from the spiritual laws booklet and explain his or her need for a Savior. "Where do you think you are on this path?" I would ask before offering to pray for the person to know Jesus. It still amazes me that a number of them said that I could pray for them; but the thing was, I never saw those people again. They avoided me, as I was a religious nut who had no idea how to relate to them, and so they had no idea how to relate to me.

From Water to Worship

After reading about that frightening method of how *not* to evangelize, let's have a look at how Jesus did it and get to grips with some practicalities of evangelism that might make it less scary for us all.

A great example of what Jesus did can be seen in John 4. Jesus is walking through Samaria and, tired from His journey, stops by a well to rest: "When a Samaritan woman came to draw water, Jesus said to her, 'Will you give me a drink?'" (v. 7). To anyone living in that day, there would be many things wrong with this picture. Jesus was breaking all cultural and social boundaries by talking to her. To start with, there was the fact that she was a woman, and devout Jews would not have begun a private conversation with a woman. Second, she was a Samaritan. We tend to associate the word "good" with Samaritan these days, so let us not forget that things would have been very different then, as the Samaritans were not a popular bunch. As if these two things weren't enough of an obstacle, it's easy to tell that this woman was considered a very bad character and an outcast from respectable society. All the women drew water during the cool of the early morning or evening, but this woman was alone, getting water in the heat of the day, probably so that she could avoid the other women who knew her reputation and wouldn't want to be seen with her.

Jesus engages her in conversation. A good point to note here with regard to striking up a conversation about Jesus with someone is to start where they are. Jesus didn't wade in with an explanation about who He was or why He had to come to Earth to live and die and reconcile us to God; He started with talking about the water she was there to draw from the well. Put simply: "Will you give Me a drink?" confused the woman because to share a drinking cup with her would have made Jesus ceremonially unclean.

Then Jesus confuses her further: "If you knew the gift of God and who it is that asks you for a drink, you would have asked him and he would have given you living water . . . whoever drinks the water I give him will never thirst" (John 4:10,14). The woman eagerly asks for the water that will quench her thirst, and Jesus replies, "Go, call your husband and come back" (v. 16). Here we find out what Jesus already knew: The woman had five husbands, which is a fair few more than her allotted quota. When she hears Jesus speaking words of truth into her life, she recognizes that He is a prophet, and so it is she who brings the subject around to worship in verse 20: "Our fathers worshiped on this mountain, but you Jews claim that the place where we must worship is in Jerusalem."

Using the Gift of Prophecy

Although Jesus had insight into the Samaritan woman's life, He didn't announce with pointed finger and raised eyebrow, "I am the Son of God. My Father has just given Me a full update on your sexual immorality, and I have a few things to say." The gift of prophecy can be a powerful tool in our evangelism, but sometimes it feels as though we've forgotten how to use it.

A friend of mine, Blaine Cook, told me how one day he was walking through a local park during his lunch hour. He saw a woman seated on a bench and he felt that God was saying to him, "She's lonely and needs a friend. Go and talk to her about Me." Knowing that he had to respond, Blaine approached her with his heart in his mouth and asked her if she was lonely and needed a friend. Tears sprang to her eyes and she said yes. "Can I tell you about Jesus?" he asked. With her permission, he began to tell her about a Friend who could relieve her loneliness, and sure enough a few weeks later she committed her life to the Lord.

Of course, Blaine took a risk in trusting that he'd heard God's voice, but that risk paid off. He even asked the woman a while later, "If I had been wrong when I sat down and asked if you were lonely, what would you have thought of me?" "I would have thought you cared," she replied. So often we worry about making mistakes and about what people will think of us if we do; but maybe there's a lesson to learn here in humbly approaching people, knowing that if at worst we are wrong, they will at least know that someone cared enough to ask.

The idea of walking up to someone you've never met and offering him or her a word from God can seem like a scary prospect, but it's not the only way to use the gift of prophecy in evangelism. With the woman at the well, for example, Jesus first said, "Go, call your husband and come back," which brought the conversation around to what He knew about her. We can pray for our friends and see if God says anything to us, but we don't then need to announce it in "Thus sayeth the Lord" fashion. We can just bring the conversation around to the area in which we feel God has given us insight, allow our friends the opportunity to open up and talk about it, and maybe offer to pray for them.

Sometimes when we try to explain to people who don't know God how and why we think God speaks, this can detract from them hearing what God is trying to say. Prophecy must be carefully, gently and lovingly handled so that we don't cause offence. It is a God-given tool that we shouldn't forget to use outside of the church.

Divine Encounters

Was it by chance that Jesus encountered the woman at the well? Was it by chance that Blaine saw the woman during his lunch break? People often talk about "divine appointments" (and it's not just a term my personal assistant uses when I turn up at the right place on the right day at the right time). We use this term to mean an encounter that God has planned in advance for us. I wonder if we would all have more divine encounters if we had our eyes open and looked for them each day. Life is busy and we tend to rush around from one thing to the next, but I believe that the more open we are, the more opportunities we will see to share God's love with people. Why not take a few minutes every now and then to look around and pray quietly for God's power and presence to fall? We often think we have to create opportunities ourselves, but the best way to find these opportunities is to follow the lead of the Holy Spirit. When we force people to listen to us or push tracts to read into their hands, it's often hard work that yields few results. We need to ask God to open doors for us rather than try to break them down ourselves with a sledgehammer.

How about making a habit of praying every morning and asking God, "Who do You want me to talk to, to love, or to serve today?" Inviting the Holy Spirit to make us aware of those He puts across our path for a reason makes us more attentive to moments that we might otherwise miss.

In soccer, for example, the best strikers are the ones who stay alert around the penalty area for the full 90 minutes of the game so that when an opening comes they are ready to put the ball in the back of the net. There are also strikers who wander around aimlessly and get out of position—when the ball comes their way they are not ready and they miss key opportunities. We need to remember to be alert to possibilities, to keep our eyes open and to be ready at all times.

Notice that in the encounter with the woman at the well, although Jesus exposed her sin, He also gave her dignity: "You are right when you say you have no husband. The fact is, you have had five husbands, and the man you now have is not your husband. What you have just said is quite true" (John 4:17-18). Though He knew that what she was doing was wrong and was ultimately causing her great pain, He didn't wade in with condemnation; He spoke kindly to her. Again we see that Jesus' motivation was not to add another faceless person to the Book of Life but to love the individual.

Rather than hiring the local town hall for an all-trumpets-blaring crusade, Jesus chose to stay with the individual, and this woman got the honor of being the first person to testify about Him. In fact, Jesus didn't need to go to the town, because once the people heard about His meeting with the Samaritan woman, they came and found Him. The testimony of one who has been healed, loved and touched by Jesus is powerful.

But I'm Not an Evangelist . . .

Says who? When Jesus gave the Great Commission to make disciples of every people group, He didn't give anyone an exemption note. We are all God's representatives, and we preach something with our lives whether we intend to or not. If you choose to stay away from non-Christians, they are likely to believe that God has no interest in them. If you choose to judge them, they will think that God only judges them. But if you choose to love them, they may just start to believe that God loves them too. We can't leave it up to the main-stage evangelists. Sure there are some people who have an amazing anointing to preach and lead people to the Lord, but if you think about the people who come to evangelistic events, where did they come from? Few wander in from the street by chance. Most are brought by friends or family members who have loved them and prayed for them for years. They may make a commitment at a big event, but they would never have gotten there if it weren't for the other evangelists in their lives.

A Few Practical Tips

Let's look at a few basic principles and practicalities of evangelism that might make it seem a bit less daunting. First, considering Jesus as our example, sometimes we forget that while being the Son of God, He also lived many elements of His life in a very normal fashion. Jesus built relationships with people. He was sociable, choosing to have dinner with those He called to follow Him, to go to parties and meet people. He didn't stay in a holy huddle with a few "safe" friends. The best thing we can do is follow Jesus' example—to see people as people and not as potential converts, to care for individuals and not worry about getting our numbers up.

Don't leave your personality at home. Because we are all made with different personalities, we all have different ways of communicating. In evangelism, as in any other area of our life, I believe that Jesus uses who we are and the things that are natural to our personality type to communicate with others. If you love people and have a passion for them to know Jesus, but can't bear the thought of talking to a crowd, then it's unlikely that God will call you to a ministry of preaching to hundreds of non-Christians. Of course that doesn't mean you're not called to be an evangelist. Some people love wading in and talking to a sales person in a store about how his or her day is going, in the hope of getting a good conversation started. If that thought makes you want to curl up into yourself and never set foot in a store again, perhaps that's not for you, but if that idea excites you, then make it a regular practice and pray that God would give you great opportunities to speak His words in those situations.

Some of the most effective evangelists are those whose main qualification is that they are great at just being friends with people. They love people for who they are; they keep in touch and call or e-mail regularly; they remember details about the other person's life and ask how things are going.

Doing evangelism isn't rocket science. Jesus wants you to relate to others as you are. We've often thought that evangelism means doing things that make us cringe, but if it's making you feel like that then imagine how it's making the other person feel! Sometimes we're pushed out of our comfort zone, and that is no bad thing, but we shouldn't make people feel awkward or force them into conversations they clearly don't want to have.

Remember what your job is and what it isn't. One of the reasons we get frustrated is because we set goals we can't achieve. You can't set out to "save" somebody, because you have no power to do that. Your job is to love, and God's is to save. You can't do His job, but you do need Him to be able to do yours. What you can achieve is being the best friend you can possibly be and to love and treat people how Jesus would, so make that your goal and bring it prayerfully before God.

Choosing Friends

I'm not really going to teach you how to make friends; I just want to remind you of what you already know. When you start to hang out with someone and find that you have fun together and share similar interests—any Manchester United supporter is a friend to me—you work out whether this person is someone you want in your life. Easy! So when you're making friends with non-Christians, the same rules apply. Love must be genuine. People can see through insincerity, and nothing is more off-putting than if you're spending time with them as a project.

If you're going to be in it for the long haul (which is what we all should be aiming for), then you need to have friends you're happy to journey with. And I'm not saying that we should only love people who are easy to love. God calls us to love everyone.

Finding Friends

Many of us already have people who don't know Jesus in our lives, whether they are friends, family, neighbors, work colleagues or fellow students. But some of us want to get to know more people, or we have a heart for a particular group to become Christians.

At Soul Survivor Watford, we've undertaken a number of initiatives over the years in order to make genuine and lasting friendships with the young people in the area. We started off with Dreggs—a café run every Friday night with live music, a relaxed atmosphere and café-style food. As the mix of people changed along with our facilities, we were able to turn this into a dance venue. We learned many things along the way about what worked and what didn't, but we tried to always put on events that achieved the aim of helping us build relationships with young people in the area. If the music got so loud we couldn't talk to people, then we turned it down. If people weren't coming because it wasn't their thing, then we tried to adapt it to attract these people again. The point was to build lasting relationships and to provide somewhere that was a stepping-stone to going to church.

We started off by going into schools and letting the students know that we were putting on a free event where they were welcome to hang out. We told them we were Christians, but promised we wouldn't preach at them. In fact, I threatened the whole team that if I caught anyone bringing up Jesus before they were asked, I would personally persecute them for many years to come! We saw our role as simply that of befriending people. As we did that, people really opened up and began to ask us about our faith.

One night we held a '70s disco, and everyone got dressed up—sideburns, flares and all—and I saw two girls, one from the school and one from our team, wearing exactly the same outfit. Being as tactful as I am, I went up to them and said, "That's pretty embarrassing that you're dressed the same." "Not at all," replied the schoolgirl proudly. "We planned it." As it turns out, a member of our team had made friends with her and they'd spent the last few evenings choosing material and then making up outfits that were identical. This same girl was one of the first to become a Christian through Dreggs. Yes, it was because we told her about Jesus; but because one of our team members cared enough to spend time with her making an outfit for a disco night, we had the relationship and thus the right to tell her.

Being part of Dreggs also made the young people feel as though they had some ownership of the church meetings. When they first decided they wanted to come to church, they would walk in and see the same décor they'd seen in the café on Friday night. "It doesn't look like church; it looks like Dreggs," they'd say. Then they would see that the same band that had been doing covers of modern songs in a café setting were now leading others in worship. They felt comfortable with us because they already had a relationship with us. They knew that they belonged, which gave them a sense of ownership. What we were trying to do was build a bridge between the church and the unchurched people in the area, to walk across the bridge to them and then walk back with them by our side, because that's what we understand to be the principle of relational evangelism.

Be open about your faith, but don't push people. Being someone's friend means that you respect their wishes just as you want them to respect yours. If you try to force-feed someone the gospel, you're unlikely to win them to salvation but highly likely to make them sick and damage your friendship in the process. There's no formula of when or how to talk about Jesus. Of course it's vital that we're open about our faith, but this can come up in natural ways. For example, "What did you do over the weekend?" is a fairly common question on a Monday morning. Mentioning that you went to church on Sunday is a non-threatening way to let people know about your faith. If they ask more, go with it, and if they don't, then leave it at that. Don't feel as though you have to make big announcements in a holy voice to get people's attention.

Listen

There are many reasons why the Alpha study courses our ministry uses have worked so well and been so effective, and one of them is that people are given the opportunity to have their say. The idea is that they can discuss what they think rather than just sitting and being told what we in the Church think. People want to be heard, and unless we listen carefully, we won't fully understand where our friends and family are coming from.

Every person's journey is different. It's all very well if you meet a friend who is armed with all the answers on evolution versus creation, but if your friend wants to know about what proof we have that Jesus exists, it's not much good, is it?

People don't expect you to have all the answers just because you're a Christian. So why bluff your way through rather than be honest and say, "You know, I'm not sure I know enough about that to give you a good answer, but I'm really happy to find out some more for you if you'd like"? Buy them a book or a tape on tricky subjects if they're genuinely interested and don't feel as though you have to have all the answers (because let's face it, we never will). People usually respect you more for saying you're not sure than when you pretend to know and understand things that you don't.

Pray

This seems obvious, but don't forget to involve God! Pray for your friends' salvation as well as for God's hand of blessing on their lives. Sometimes it's appropriate to let someone know if you're praying for him or her over a particular situation. More people are touched in a positive way by your praying than you would imagine. Again, the key thing is to handle prayer sensitively and be respectful of their wishes.

So maybe evangelism is not so scary after all! When we know that our basic qualification for evangelism is to love God and those who don't know Him, the idea is a lot less daunting. If we've felt disheartened that people aren't interested in God anymore, then we need to remember that it's not that He is outdated in today's culture, but that maybe the methods we've used to communicate His message are. We don't need to set ourselves challenges that only lead to a fall, like trying to convert whole cities in one weekend using the latest evangelism strategy. We just need to follow Jesus' example to see people as individuals, not judging them but building genuine and lasting relationships and being committed to them simply because we love them.

The Question of Suffering

I've often found that one of the first questions that non-Christians will ask about my faith is, "If this God of yours is so loving and powerful, why is there so much suffering in the world?"

If only there were a succinct 3-point, 30-second answer that we could memorize to help us out of that spot! Part of the question people are asking is, "Does God care?" and we know that the answer is a resounding yes! Most people may never pick up a Bible long enough to see just how passionate God is about ending pain and suffering, so ours may be the only voice they hear in answer to that question. The way we respond can't just be in words. We know that God could come and bring justice and remove suffering in an instant, but He chooses to use us to tell others about Him. One of the most effective ways of letting people outside of the Church see God's heart for this world is if we, His people, who represent Him on Earth, go out and demonstrate it with our lives.

PART 3

Justice

God's Heart for Justice

The word "justice" seems to be a buzzword in today's culture, with pop stars and politicians alike proclaiming the needs of the world. This is great and can make a real difference, but what happens in a few years when it's no longer fashionable to be talking about it? For Christians there's no option for justice to be in or out of style; we should be committed to justice as a way of life because it is one of the key expressions of God's heart. The Bible is absolutely clear that God is passionate about how the poor, the oppressed, the marginalized and the dispossessed are treated.

> The righteous care about justice for the poor,
> but the wicked have no such concern (Prov. 29:7).

It's often been said that if God says something once in the Bible, He means it; and if He says it twice, he *really* means it. So if I tell you that this subject warrants 500 verses of direct teaching in the New Testament alone, you'd probably rub a few brain cells together and conclude that justice is something that is pretty close to God's heart. In fact, I'd go so far as to say He is completely and utterly passionate about it. We often worry about things like the Second Coming, sexual immorality and the nature of heaven and hell; but there's something else higher up on God's agenda. It's how we handle our money and how we treat the poor, the oppressed and the marginalized. In fact, the only topic that has more teachings devoted to it in the whole of the Bible is idolatry.

One in 16 New Testament verses, and one in 12 in the Gospels, speaks about God's passion for the poor. What does that tell us? If we were to cut out the verses of the Bible that talk about how we deal with our money and possessions in light of the poor, then all we'd be left with is a Bible full of holes. Could it be that for many years we have been ignoring this issue and preaching from the tattered remains of what is left of our Bibles? We've often gotten hung up on things that Jesus didn't spend that much time talking about and, thus, we have often overlooked the very heartbeat of God.

It's not just the number of times the Bible talks about these things; it's also the passion with which God speaks about them. Take this passage from Isaiah 58, for example. This is one passage that doesn't need a skilled Bible teacher to bring out the meaning; it could not be more clear. The people have been complaining that they have been upholding their religious duties, and yet God's ears seem to be closed to their prayers. God's response is passionate and direct, and you can find it in Isaiah 58:5-12.

> Do you think this is the kind of fast day I'm after:
> a day to show off humility?
> To put on a pious long face
> and parade around solemnly in black?
> Do you call that fasting,
> a fast day that I, God, would like?
> (*THE MESSAGE*).

God is angry that they spend all their time worrying about the outward appearance of righteousness and yet have little regard for what it really means to be holy and for how God wants them to act. They have separated the spiritual from the secular; they keep the law religiously, make a great show of fasting, but then exploit their workers. God doesn't leave them to second-guess what's important to Him and what He's really after. He makes it clear: You can't keep up this show of being My followers without acting on the things I am passionate about.

> This is the kind of fast day I'm after:
> to break the chains of injustice,
> get rid of exploitation in the workplace,
> free the oppressed,
> cancel debts.
> What I'm interested in seeing you do is:
> sharing your food with the hungry,
> inviting the homeless poor into your homes,
> putting clothes on the shivering ill-clad,
> being available to your own families
> (Isa. 58:6, *THE MESSAGE*).

These are the issues God cares about—not whether we wear black when we are fasting but whether we love Him enough to look after those in need. He wants to know that our hearts are moved by people's plights and that we follow through with action.

As I said earlier, when we give to God, He can't seem to help but give back to us. In the following passage of Scripture, He makes great promises to His people. This is an amazing example of God's grace—they were really messing up and getting it wrong, yet God was willing to make wonderful pledges of goodness to them if they would turn again to His ways. Isn't that amazing? When I look at my own life and remember the countless times I've sung the songs but not lived the life, I thank God that I can always start over and that it's never too late to try to get it right.

Do this and the lights will turn on,
and your lives will turn around at once.
Your righteousness will pave your way.
The God of glory will secure your passage.
Then when you pray, God will answer.
You'll call out for help and I'll say, "Here I am."
If you get rid of unfair practices,
quit blaming victims,
quit gossiping about other people's sins,
If you are generous with the hungry
and start giving yourselves to the down-and-out,
Your lives will begin to glow in the darkness,
your shadowed lives will be bathed in sunlight.
I will always show you where to go.
I'll give you a full life in the emptiest of places—
firm muscles, strong bones.
You'll be like a well-watered garden,
a gurgling spring that never runs dry.
You'll use the old rubble of past lives to build anew,
rebuild the foundations from out of your past.
You'll be known as those who can fix anything,

restore old ruins, rebuild and renovate,
make the community livable again
(Isa. 58:8-12, *THE MESSAGE*).

In this passage God promises that He will answer their prayers again if they let love infiltrate and motivate all areas of their lives. The principle is the same as Jesus preached: that if we try to keep our lives, we will lose them, but if we are willing to turn all areas of our lives over to Him and die to ourselves, we will gain true life.

Throughout the Old Testament the prophets often delivered the same message: You're upholding the religious practices, but you're forgetting the heart of it so that they have become empty rituals. For example, Micah says:

With what shall I come before the Lord
and bow down before the exalted God?
Shall I come before him with burnt offerings,
with calves a year old?
Will the Lord be pleased with thousands of rams,
with ten thousand rivers of oil?
Shall I offer my firstborn for my transgression,
the fruit of my body for the sin of my soul?
He has showed you, O man, what is good.
And what does the Lord require of you?
To act justly and to love mercy
and to walk humbly with your God
(Mic. 6:6-8).

The prophet clearly makes his point. Is God only pleased with huge, extravagant sacrifices like a thousand rivers of oil? Is the only way to please Him to sacrifice the most precious thing we have besides Him, our own children? No. God has made Himself clear: We are to "act justly and to love mercy and to walk humbly" with Him. Over the next few chapters we will look at what it might mean for us to act justly and love mercy, because it is clear that this is something we cannot afford to miss.

What Do We Mean When We Talk About the Poor and Injustice?

It's easy to see "the poor" as a term for those who don't have enough money; but we also need to include in this definition those who suffer physically, mentally, spiritually, emotionally and socially. Often, many of these elements are combined and are catalysts for each other. We can't say that poverty is something that only affects the developing world, as people on our very doorsteps, no matter where we live, may be poor in one form or another. We're talking not only about those who live below the financial poverty line but also about those who have been abused (physically, mentally and emotionally), those who have lost their homes and possessions through wars and natural disasters, those who are lonely or bullied, those who are suffering from illness or addiction. The list goes on.

These situations are all unjust in the sense that they are not how things would be if God's kingdom ruled. But there is also another sense of injustice in the world: "Injustice occurs when power is misused to take from others what God has given them, namely their life, dignity, liberty or the fruits of their love or labor."[1] Examples of some of the ongoing injustices in our world today are abusive child labor, forced prostitution, corrupt police and governing bodies, child pornography, racial violence, terrorism and imprisonment without fair trial. The list seems endless.

The Bible makes it clear that doing something about this injustice is part of our worship to God: "He who oppresses the poor shows contempt for their Maker, but whoever is kind to the needy honors God" (Prov. 14:31). If we do not take justice seriously, we are not taking God and His ways seriously. If we want to truly honor God, we must stop seeing worship as something we do in church, and take it out into society.

Giving and Generosity

If we want to reflect God's heart and nature, we also have to know that He is a generous God and act accordingly.

Even though we know that the subject of money is one among many other areas of life that we handle better when we're accountable to someone about it, we're not very good at talking about money. As Christians we're happy to ask our friends how their relationship with God is; we have people who will regularly check in with us about how we're doing with our Bible reading and our prayer times; and we'd be comfortable challenging someone we loved who wasn't attending church. But when it comes to money, we get shy and embarrassed and don't want to pry. Even in the most honest of accountability relationships, we rarely challenge each other or dare to ask where the money goes. Maybe it's because the saying is true that the last part of us to be converted is usually our wallets.

When we talk about the poor, often our first reaction is to think, *Well, I'm not exactly rich.* We look at celebrities who spend millions on numerous mansions around the globe, have their own private jets to fly them wherever they like, are never seen in the same item of clothing twice, and think nothing of buying jewelry for the price of a small country, and we think, *I can barely afford a new pair of running shoes!* We don't consider ourselves rich, yet we're able to keep our food in a refrigerator and have a closet to put our clothes in, a roof over our heads and a bed to sleep in at night. These are things that we consider basics, and yet 75 percent of the world's population doesn't have these luxuries, which means that if you have all of those things, you are in the top 25 percent of wealthy people in the entire world.

If you shrank the world proportionally into 100 people, only 8 of them would have a computer and 4 would have an Internet connection. The Internet is again something we can easily take for granted. Those of us who are lucky enough to have access to it are in the top 4 percent of the world's richest people. It is humbling to see on a world scale how rich we truly are. (These statistics are from www.miniatureearth.com.)

The way we spend our money is often a direct reflection of what's in our hearts: "For where your treasure is, there your heart will be also" (Matt. 6:21). If someone who didn't know you picked up your bank statement, what would it tell him or her about you? Would it be clear what you're passionate about? Could this person tell how much you love shopping for clothes or the latest gadgets, going for meals with family and friends, following a favorite sporting team or musician? None of these things are in and of themselves bad things to spend money on, but they may highlight our priorities.

People often say things like, "All of our money belongs to God," which is true, but saying that doesn't provide a practical guide for knowing how to handle money. God has entrusted money to us with the aim of furthering His kingdom, and we will have to give account for how we've used that money. Can you imagine sitting down with God and the world's largest calculator, going through all the money that has passed through your possession over the entire period of your life and explaining to God how it was used to serve Him?

Again King David is a great role model for us—only this time, he shows us how to think about our ability to give: "But who am I, and who are my people, that we should be able to give as generously as this? Everything comes from you, and we have given you only what comes from your hand" (1 Chron. 29:14). David realized that it all comes from God and that it's a privilege to be able to give generously to God's work.

Traditionally in churches we pass around a plate when it's time to take up the collection, and we sing a hymn along with it. We changed how we do this in our church after I saw the way the people in a poor township church in South Africa gave their money. They had so little and yet their giving was like an explosion of joy. They came out of their seats, singing and dancing and praising God with all their might as they brought their gifts to baskets at the front. There was nothing passive or apathetic about their giving. They were so happy to be able to do it and were some of the most generous people I have ever come across, despite their poverty.

We read in 2 Corinthians 9:6-7: "Whoever sows sparingly will also reap sparingly, and whoever sows generously will also reap generously. Each man should give what he has decided in his heart to give, not reluctantly or under compulsion, for God loves a cheerful giver." The Greek word for "cheerful" can alternatively be translated "hilarious"; God is looking for generous people who take joy in giving and are extravagant with Him.

Tithing

Tithing is a very important part of our giving, but giving the tithe (or tenth) shouldn't be where giving stops. It's not a case of giving Him the first 10 percent and then keeping the rest. All that we have is a gift from God that we should offer back to Him in thanksgiving for His provision: "You will be made rich in every way so that you can be generous on every occasion, and . . . your generosity will result in thanksgiving to God" (2 Cor. 9:11). God gives to us so that we can bless others. He is generous to us so that we can be generous toward those around us. Again, God's desire is not that we follow the letter of the law but the heart of it. As Jesus said, "Woe to you, teachers of the law and Pharisees, you hypocrites! You give a tenth of your spices—mint, dill and cummin. But you have neglected the more important matters of the law—justice, mercy and faithfulness. You should have practiced the latter, without neglecting the former" (Matt. 23:23).

Jesus was pointing out how hypocritical it was for the Pharisees to tithe on even their tiniest of garden herbs and yet not look after the poor. They were following their religious duty, but they were not honoring God as their Provider and using all that He had given to be generous to those in need. God is always interested in what is going on in our hearts. Do we desire money and financial security over Him or are we able to be generous and live in His freedom?

Right after Jesus teaches us that we "cannot serve both God and Money" (Matt. 6:24), He reminds us why we don't need to get hung up about finances:

> Therefore I tell you, do not worry about your life, what you will eat or drink; or about your body, what you will wear. Is not life more important than food, and the body more important than clothes? . . . So do not worry . . . your heavenly Father knows that you need them. But seek first his kingdom and his righteousness, and all these things will be given to you as well (Matt. 6:25,31-33).

There is an amazing freedom in knowing that we are under God's protection and care. We need to live in a way that reflects the fact that we know we have a God who loves and cares for us, who, with all the resources in heaven and on earth at His disposal, is more than capable of meeting our every need. If we truly believe that, we won't worry about living generously with our time, our money and our possessions and following God's call wherever He may lead. We love others because we are so overwhelmed by His great love for us. We go to those who have nothing, knowing that as we pursue the kingdom of God, He will take care of our needs.

CHAPTER EIGHT

Compassion for a Broken World

Although there is more than enough food for everyone in the world, 800 million people do not have enough to eat.[1] Forty million people are currently living with AIDS/HIV virus, and 2.5 million of these are children.[2] In Africa, 13.4 million children have been orphaned by HIV.[3] Every single day 30,000 children die as a result of extreme poverty—despite the fact that we have the knowledge, the resources and the opportunity to end this.[4] The developing world now spends $13 on debt repayment for every $1 it receives in grants.[5] In Africa more than 2 million infants die each year without reaching their fifth birthday.[6] Eighty-five out of 100 people in the world don't have running water at home;[7] 1.4 million children die each year from lack of access to safe drinking water and adequate sanitation.[8]

In 2004, 24 percent of children in England and Wales were living in single-parent families.[9] Also, in England and Wales the people most likely to die a violent death are babies under one year old, who are four times more likely to be killed than the average person.[10] Around 140,000 people in the UK attempt to commit suicide each year.[11]

The state of the world can be overwhelming. We look at these statistics and they begin to blur; our minds don't know how to process this kind of information. But these statistics are not just numbers; they represent people, God's creation. Each one of those babies who dies before reaching the age of five was knit together in his or her mother's womb, fearfully and wonderfully made (see Ps. 139:13-14). Each one of the men, women and children who goes to sleep hungry at night bears God's image. Jesus' promise that we could have life to the full was for every one of the almost 6,000 adults who committed suicide last year in the UK because life seemed so painful and hopeless to them.[12]

Cultivating Hearts of Compassion

The first and most important thing to understand about growing a more compassionate heart is the necessity of getting close to God. As we know Him more, we begin to share His heart and become aware of His ways. In Matthew 22, Jesus is asked about the most important commandment, and He says, "'Love the Lord your God with all your heart and with all your soul and with all your mind.' This is the first and greatest commandment. And the second is like it: 'Love your neighbor as yourself'" (vv. 37-39).

There are five important words I want to pull out: "the second is like it." We usually separate these two commands; we know they are our top priorities, but we feel that they are surely quite different instructions. Not according to Jesus.

Loving our brother is a vital part of loving God. As the apostle John says, "If anyone says, 'I love God,' yet hates his brother, he is a liar. For anyone who does not love his brother, whom he has seen, cannot love God, whom he has not seen. . . . Whoever loves God must also love his brother" (1 John 4:20-21).

We must act compassionately as a result of having had a revelation of God's heart, otherwise we are doing just what anyone with a big heart and no knowledge of God can do. The closer and more intimate we get with God, the more we recognize our selfish and self-indulgent ways and begin to share His heart for others.

Sometimes we have to choose not to turn away from the pain in the world. With so many channels on the TV, we're used to just flicking over to the next station when the viewing doesn't suit us. We come home after a hard day at work or college classes and think, "I can't face seeing those poor starving children again" or "The news just depresses me. I think I'll watch something else." It is often a difficult and conscious choice to watch and hear about another senseless murder, a new part of the world reeling from a natural disaster, miscarriages of justice, or the growth of diseases like HIV. It's far easier to switch over and watch something more palatable—perhaps a soap opera, where problems are resolved easily and then quickly forgotten—rather than seeing real issues. But if we want to expand our hearts, sometimes we need to turn back and watch prayerfully, to share the Father's pain about the state of the world, to listen and see what we can do and to think about our response.

Because the truth is, if we don't look properly, we'll never cultivate a true heart of compassion. If we want our hearts to be changed, then we need to get involved. Often I think we're afraid to see things fully because we know that once we have, we can never plead ignorance to God; we'll have blown that excuse out of the water.

After the first time I saw the pictures of starving people in Ethiopia in the 1980s, I knew God could call me to account at the end of my days; He could ask, "How did your life change after you saw that? You felt the Holy Spirit tugging at your heart—did you squash Him or allow Him to open up your heart and lead you to action?"

The trouble is, even pictures on the TV have become almost meaningless. We've become so used to seeing pictures of starving people on our screens and then turning over to see images of celebrity lifestyles, that both are equally unreal to us. We need some spiritual heart surgery to awaken us again to the pain in the world, and often the best way to do this is to see it for ourselves. Statistics are hard to relate to—we need to see the people behind the statistics to cultivate hearts of compassion.

John Stott suggested that one of the best ways to pray is to hold your Bible in one hand and a newspaper in the other. We have to see what's going on in the world and what the Bible says about it and about how we should respond.

The thing that stretched my heart more than anything and made me realize I couldn't turn away any longer was meeting the street children from South Africa that I told you about at the start of this book. Meeting them changed my heart in a way that reading about them or seeing pictures on the TV never could. Seeing a friend stand before you weak with hunger—who wouldn't buy him or her food? If someone you cared about needed a doctor, you would do everything in your power to make sure that person got the needed medical attention. That's how we respond when we're motivated by compassion and love, and when people become real to us rather than just statistics.

There are thousands of children like my friends in South Africa all over the world. These are children who have none of the things we take for granted: the love of a family who will take care of us, the security of a home, the expectation that if we are hurting or ill we will be able to get treatment, and the ability to wash so that we can feel clean and decent every day.

The God I know is brokenhearted over what we've allowed to happen to some of His children. Justice today is to say, "Your kingdom come, your will be done on earth as it is in heaven" (Matt. 6:10).

Of course you don't have to look past your own street to find people who are hurting and in need of love and support. One of my friends, Emily, moved with three others to a house in an average suburban town and decided to see what she could do to bless the lives of her neighbors. Here is her story:

> When we moved in we found there was a woman living next door with four children between 4 and 11. Her husband (father to three of them) would come and go depending on whether he'd found another woman to be with, so there wasn't a lot of stability in the house. He was also a drug dealer and saw nothing wrong in showing the kids how to burgle from others; it was a regular thing for one of them to be in trouble with the police.
>
> Domestic violence was commonplace in the household; the parents would shout at and hit the kids on a daily basis and throw things at each other during screaming rows. Unsurprisingly, the kids were violent and aggressive themselves; to them, this was just a normal way to express feelings, but it got them in lots of trouble. The eldest was suspended from school for violent behavior at the age of 11, and the youngest was almost

expelled for a vicious attack on an older pupil—she was just 5 years old at the time.

Their mother struggled to help them with even the basics; she didn't know how to cook, so she would send the kids around to the chip shop each night to get their tea (when they saw fruit and vegetables at our house they couldn't tell us what they were). She was illiterate and couldn't help them with their homework and hadn't even taught them how to brush their teeth or to wash their hands after going to the toilet.

One of the things we found hardest to see was the emotional abuse they suffered. They were constantly told they were useless, that there was no hope for them, they would amount to nothing and would end up in prison. They even called one of them "the child of the devil."

Because of all of this, the kids craved adult attention and affirmation. We knew that if we wanted to help, we had to commit to being part of these children's lives. There was no point in giving them money or just taking them on the odd day out to get a break; we wanted to be a positive influence on the whole of their lives.

Thus, we invited them into our house and said they could come over whenever they wanted. We showed them how to cook and taught them about basic nutrition. We took them to the park, taught them about hygiene, helped with their homework (we even had to teach the eldest boy, who was by then 13, what the letters of the alphabet were and the months of the year). We took them to Sunday School and tried to affirm them, to find out what they were good at and encourage them to develop their gifts; we explained why school was a positive thing and how it could open up opportunities for them in the future.

We let them do jobs for us around the house to earn money and showed them how to do a basic invoice so that they could start learning some job skills. We also tried really hard to get to know the parents, to invite them around for a drink and to build a relationship and a trust with them too. The mum used to come around if her husband had left her again or if she felt she needed a refuge from him when he was in a violent temper.

It was hard work and sometimes we would get fed up or just worn out. It was disheartening when they stole from us, but we'd try to keep reminding each other why we had chosen to get involved.

We did see huge changes in them too; one of them still comes to church. Five years after we moved into town, they softened and began to trust us (not an easy thing for them). They had better social skills and so began to make friends; they started regularly attending school and they managed to stay out of trouble with the police.

Who Are We to Change Anything?

The trouble with looking at the state of the world is that it can overwhelm us. Things can look so bleak that we lose hope and feel small and helpless in the face of the atrocities we witness.

It seems as though any effort we could make wouldn't make even the smallest dent, never mind much of an impact. For every family that we can get involved with, like Emily and her friends did, aren't there hundreds more that we can do nothing about? The absolute worst thing we can do is to let this feeling of helplessness paralyze us.

When a journalist asked U2's Bono about his work in Africa and why he thought he could make a difference, he replied, "We can't lose because we're putting our shoulder to a door that God Almighty has already opened."[13] And that's the truth of it. This is God's idea first. This is God's agenda, and I believe He will lead, guide and help us as we go.

I was encouraged and inspired to read in *Good News About Injustice* by Gary A. Haugen about a number of Christians who brought about huge changes for justice through their faithful walks with God. In the late 1800s, for example, Kate Bushnell, an evangelical Christian, was devastated to see many girls being forced into prostitution in Wisconsin. With the police turning a blind eye and the doctors encouraging these rapes due to the additional income of examining the injured girls, Kate was fighting a tough battle. Putting herself at great physical risk, she undertook investigative work and presented her evidence until people were forced to take notice. Eventually a bill was passed in her name that put an end to this horrendous practice.

It seems almost impossible to imagine it now, but at the beginning of the last century enforced child labor was still a serious issue in North America. Edgar Murphy was a minister from Alabama who began writing about the horrors he had seen. He distributed copies of his reports throughout the United States (often funded from his own pocket) in order to raise awareness of what was happening. Murphy was a founding member of the committee whose work brought about the abolition of child slavery.

Both of these cases would have looked to be almost impossible battles to fight before Kate Bushnell and Edgar Murphy took up their causes. I'm sure there were many times they both doubted the effectiveness of what they were doing and whether or not they could really make a difference. No doubt there were great personal sacrifices along the way—money, time, safety and reputation—yet they stayed true to God's heart and, in doing so, changed the lives of many millions of people.

William Booth is another exemplary figure in the fight for justice. He was the founder of the Salvation Army. A Methodist minister in the 1800s, he realized there was a large part of society that the Church wasn't reaching. So he took his preaching from the pulpit to the poor and spent himself on telling them about the love of Jesus. From this humble start grew the organization that today operates in over 100 countries around the world and serves millions of people each year. They run many initiatives to give practical help, from homeless shelters to hospitals, addiction centers to community youth programs, and counseling to education centers. What started as a desire in one man's heart to reach the lost became an international mission that is bearing fruit almost 100 years after his death; it will no doubt continue to do so for many more years.

There are many stories that encourage us that one person's faith can impact the world. I'm sure there are countless more Christians whose stories have never been told but whose day-today living and desire to follow God has made a radical difference and changed people's lives and futures. We're not in it for the glory, but we should take to heart that each seed God sows in our hearts, if nurtured and acted on, can yield more fruit than we could possibly imagine.

God's Promise of Blessing

God doesn't promise us that the fight for justice will be easy—there is a great cost involved—but He does promise us that He will be with us and reward us. One verse I have always loved is Proverbs 19:17: "He who is kind to the poor lends to the Lord." What an idea! That we can give God a gift and that we can lend something to Him by being kind to those who have less than we do. The end of the sentence isn't bad either: "and he will reward him for what he has done." Again we see this truth that as we give to God, we see more of His generosity and blessings in our own lives.

God doesn't make this promise just once. Take a look at these verses:

A generous man will himself be blessed,
for he shares his food with the poor (Prov. 22:9).

Give, and it will be given to you. A good measure,
pressed down, shaken together and running over, will
be poured into your lap. For with the measure you use,
it will be measured to you (Luke 6:38).

It is clear that this is God's way. He is a generous God and He wants our lives to reflect His generosity. We have to be careful, however, that we don't make assumptions about what God's blessing will look like. Sometimes we look at it like the ultimate fail-safe "get rich quick" scheme: We give away and God gives us back more. Bingo! But we know it doesn't really work like that because God knows that earthly riches are not the highest reward He can give. Yes, He often does bless us with money and financial provision, wonderful homes and promotions at work, but as we give our hearts, our time, our money and our possessions, we may find that the blessing we receive is rather a closer understanding of God's presence in our daily walk. It may be that we notice a change in our hearts and attitudes, an increased peace and lack of worry over His provision because we know that we are in safe hands. He might want to bless us with a heart that aches for a broken world, being humble enough to count serving God in any capacity and at any cost a privilege, or being abandoned to the idea that possessions count for little and that pleasing God counts for a lot.

Good will come to him who is generous and lends freely, who conducts his affairs with justice (Ps. 112:5).

CHAPTER NINE

What Can I Do?

So we've talked about *what* justice is and how close to God's heart it is, and *why* we should take action so that our worship of God impacts all areas of our life. The next question when considering active compassion is *how?* This chapter is devoted to the practical steps we can all take to make the fight for justice part of our everyday lives.

And that's the key—it doesn't have to be about making a decision to sell all that we have and give that money to the poor, but it needs to be about building acts of justice into our lives in steps that we can manage, constantly bringing this goal before God and asking Him what else we can be doing.

Some people might be able to make radical changes and stick with them, but if you're anything like me, you'll get all excited, promise you'll change all your ways, fail within hours and then, disheartened, decide to give up. Like most areas of our lives, we start with small steps and then keep growing and developing until we can walk, jog, run and eventually go the long distance. I would really encourage you, as you read through this chapter, to think about the steps you can take. There may be loads that you are already doing, which is great, but keep going for it and keep your eyes and heart open for more.

Of course, this is not an exhaustive list—there are endless numbers of creative ways you can be fighting for justice. These are just some ideas to get you thinking.

Pray

The first thing we can all do, and should make a regular practice of doing, is to pray about the injustices in the world. We all have testimony from our own lives of the ways we have cried out to God and seen His mighty hand at work. God makes us many promises regarding prayer. For example, "will not God bring about justice for his chosen ones, who cry out to him day and night?" (Luke 18:7) and "If my people, who are called by my name, will humble themselves and pray and seek my face and turn from their wicked ways, then will I hear from heaven and will forgive their sin and will heal their land" (2 Chron. 7:14).

We may need to start praying by asking God to give us His compassion. If you don't feel it, don't try to fake it, but be honest and say, "God, I know I should care more about this than I do at the moment. Please mold my heart to long for the things You long for. Give me a desire to pray and serve and seek Your kingdom in my life."

Prayer is so much more than putting requests before God; it's about building relationship with Him. When we talk to Him and listen, we begin to share His heart. As Richard Foster said, "Prayer is the central avenue God uses to change us."[1] I don't know about you, but I know that my heart needs some changing if it is to better reflect my Father's heart for this world. We can't tackle these issues in our own strength or simply out of a sense of duty, because such acts are not sustainable long term and we'll be in danger of getting worn out, burned out and resentful. We need to be motivated from a place of love, starting with a love for our God; as we begin to share His heart,

He will give us a love for the people to whom He wants to send us.

Often during times of intercession when people begin to discover God's heart in this way, they find themselves unable to speak, and they simply weep as they share something of His pain and anguish over a broken world. They find that words just don't seem to be enough, and they are helpless to express what they feel in their hearts, so they intercede with tears. It is just like what Paul wrote to the Romans: "The Spirit helps us in our weakness. We do not know what we ought to pray for, but the Spirit himself intercedes for us with groans that words cannot express" (Rom. 8:26).

Where to Start

Many Christian charities produce free prayer guides, which can be a great place to start. They're ideal for giving you a focus, especially if there's a particular charity whose work you're interested in. They'll often send you newsletters that will keep you updated on what they're doing and the good things they've seen God do.

Watching the daily news can be a heartbreaking experience, but it is also an amazing aid to prayer. Looking through the paper or turning on the radio or TV and watching with God's eyes prompts us to ask Him to be involved in these situations, to bring about His justice, to raise up more people to tackle the issues that are rife in our world. Sometimes we feel as if we can do little more than pray for the family mourning the loss of a child who has been senselessly murdered, but there may also be times and situations when God calls us to be the very answers to the prayers we pray, because so often prayer leads to action.

Pete Greig began the powerful 24-7 prayer movement that started people around the world opening prayer rooms so that for days, weeks and months at a time there were people praying around the clock. Pete was told by Brennan Manning, author of *The Ragamuffin Gospel,* "The most powerful thing that can happen in the place of prayer is that you become the prayer. You leave the room as Jesus' hands and feet on earth."[2]

We've been realizing that there is a place for weeping over the pain and suffering in the world, and God answers prayer sometimes in the most spectacular of ways, but the truth is that the tears themselves don't feed anyone. Yes, we should cry out. Yes, we should bring this pain before God. But sometimes we have to get up and get out and be the answer to the very prayers we've prayed. We can't shout from the comfort of our churches and living rooms, "We love you," to people who need food, because the words are hollow to their ears unless they see that we are willing to share our food with them. "Suppose a brother or sister is without clothes and daily food. If one of you says to him, 'Go, I wish you well; keep warm and well fed,' but does nothing about his physical needs, what good is it?" (Jas. 2:15-16).

Give Financially

We've already talked about how important it is that we use our money to bless others, whether as part of our tithe or in addition to it. We should all be generous with the money God has given us and put it to good use. There are so many charities that would use even $5 a month to make a difference in people's lives. There's no right or wrong way to pick a charity—we all have different causes we can relate to or things that we are passionate about—so see what is in your heart and where you would like to give.

Child Sponsorship

One great way to give that has tangible results is to sponsor a child. For about $30 a month you can literally change someone's life. Sometimes it's the difference between life and death for the child. Your money provides the essentials of clean water, food, basic healthcare and immunization against disease. Often, in addition, it provides education and life-skills training courses that give people a means to generate their own income and change their future. If you're not currently earning, or not earning very much, you could make a commitment with a group of friends or your cell group and see how far your collective money will go.

Giving Charitable Gifts

It is estimated that every year $280 billion is spent on Christmas presents in the United States alone. I think it's a wonderful thing that we can express our love and appreciation for people by buying gifts, but sometimes it feels as though things get a bit out of control. We have far more than we could possibly ever need and yet we spend so much on getting even more. A number of charities have thought of a way that we could use birthdays and Christmas as an additional opportunity to bless others in need and be more outward looking in our approach to buying presents. They've launched alternative gift catalogues from which you can buy presents that could transform a life, a family or even a whole community. With prices ranging from a few dollars to a few hundred dollars, offering everything from a fruit tree that provides income and food for a family for less than the price of a CD, to a water system that will save members of a village from having to travel miles each and every day just to get water that isn't contaminated.

Fund-raising

Most of us don't have an endless supply of cash and we find it frustrating to hear of all the worthy causes that could do with more money than we can't give. Creative fund-raising could be the answer. You could do local car washes, hold a sponsored run/fast/silence/weight-loss, have a garage or yard sale, or host fund-raising dinners and parties, raffles or auctions. The possibilities are endless.

Get your church home group or youth group involved and enjoy the fun, knowing that you're doing something that will change people's lives. Through being generous with our money, we can make a huge difference in the lives of people who have very little. But God doesn't want us to seek justice only with our finances.

Shop Wisely—Buy Fair Trade

Have you ever stopped to think about your power as a consumer? Most of the time we only see ourselves as individuals and don't imagine that we can make much difference, but our buying power has a very loud voice. Companies spend millions upon millions of dollars trying to get us to buy their products. If we start "voting with our feet" and taking our business to places that have good ethical policies, then people will sit up and begin to take notice.

Be an Ethical Consumer

Nestlé is one of the world's largest companies, and in the late 1970s, it was found to be exploiting new mothers in developing countries. In response, the Infant Formula Action Coalition called for a boycott. Nestlé was offering new mothers powder from which to make a milk drink for their babies, and by the time the "free gift" had finished, the mother's own milk had dried up. This left them with only one alternative: to continue to buy the expensive powder and mix it with unclean water. This was causing many infant deaths and malnutrition. It seemed strange at first to think that you'd make much of a difference if you stopped buying their most famous brand of coffee and substituted a Cadbury's chocolate bar for a Nestlé one. But when thousands of people started to do it and the company's sales plummeted, they began to take notice. During the 1980s, the company changed its policies for the better.

Nestlé says it no longer uses such aggressive and unethical marketing policies, but organizations like International Baby Food Action Network and Baby Milk Action (www.babymilk action.org) say the company still violates agreed codes of conduct and should still be boycotted.[3]

Many companies also use child labor, pay unfair wages or force workers to toil in unreasonable conditions in order to keep their costs down and make cheap products. If we want to be ethical consumers, we should be looking at companies' policies to see whether they pay the producers a fair rate or whether they use slave labor. It's really tempting to think, *but this T-shirt's so cheap!* Don't forget that somebody somewhere always has to pay the price.

However, while boycotting worked well with Nestlé and its unethical practices, and where there are issues of slave labor, boycotting may do more harm than good to the individuals concerned. If people stop buying the products, factories may close and put people out of work. Even earning a small amount is clearly more desirable than earning nothing at all, so it is more effective for us to make our voice heard by asking to see companies' policies and make our interest in fair-trade products known.

Lobby

Speak up for those who cannot speak for themselves,
for the rights of all who are destitute.
Speak up and judge fairly;
defend the rights of the poor and needy.
Proverbs 31:8-9

In this era of mass communication and easy Internet access, lobbying has never been easier. Filling in postcards, writing letters and forwarding e-mails all add your voice to the growing number of people who are asking for governments and companies to take responsibility for bringing about justice. Charities are keen for people's support and will usually provide details of petitions you can sign, will send you free postcards to use, will provide you with draft letters, and will give you all the tools you need to speak up for those who cannot speak up for themselves.

As Martin Luther King, Jr., said, "We will have to repent in this generation not merely for the cruel words and actions of the bad people, but for the appalling silence of the good people."

Bank Wisely

Did you know that the money in your bank account could be invested in the arms trade, pornography, organizations that do not uphold basic human rights and exploit their workers, and companies that test their products on animals and damage the environment? Ask your bank about how ethical their investment policies are. If you're not happy with the answers, move your money somewhere it won't be used for harm.

Consider Short-term Missions

In a few months' time, our church, Soul Survivor Watford, is going to Durban, South Africa, for a house party. I can't tell you how excited I am that we're going as a family. We've often held house parties where God has met with us and blessed us, and I know this will be a house party that makes a difference as we look to be a blessing to that community. We're planning on having time together to meet with God and time to relax, but we intend to spend our afternoons working with the street kids in the poorest shanty town communities and at an orphanage for children whose parents have died from AIDS.

This is such an amazing opportunity for us to share in an adventure together, particularly for those of us who haven't been exposed to the kind of poverty we will encounter there. We want to be a practical blessing and have our eyes and our hearts opened to some of the suffering in our world.

There are many ways you can get involved in short-term missions, whether it's through reputable agencies or joining members of your church who need help with their missionary work. If you work with people who know the area and the problems, you can make sure that your presence is a blessing and that your efforts are directed in the best possible way.

You may want to take a gap year before, after, or during studies or work; or you may be able to give a few weeks. If you can make the time, there are certainly enough places where it could be put to good use.

Commit to Long-term Missions

There are many whose heart's desire is to be a missionary in the traditional sense of living overseas in a deprived area and working full time with those who are most in need. Friends of mine from Holland, Daniel and Marlies, have left the comforts of home for Kitale in northern Kenya to serve God among the people there. Here's what they told me:

Since we were children, we've both always had an interest in Africa and have loved the idea of living there. But at the age of 24, we were settled in Holland, had been married for four years and were working for a Christian organization. We were happy there and still felt there was plenty for us to do with the young people we were working with. After a trip to the poor region of northern Kenya, we began to feel that God was calling us to move there.

We felt so under-prepared—we'd never been to Bible college and we didn't consider ourselves to have any special skills we could offer. We were just two people who wanted to serve God wherever He called us. Our passion was the same in Kenya as it was in Holland: to see young people meet with God and make a difference in their society.

In the 18 months we've been in Kenya, so much has already happened. We've opened an orphanage that has given a home to six kids, and we have a food program for almost 100 primary school children that ensures they get at least one warm meal a day. With help from churches and organizations abroad, we've furnished a primary school, built a center for the church and community to use, given out clothes and food to local villages and are currently looking into starting a first-aid program. It sounds like a lot, but there's so much still to do. We're building a center for the young people to meet and pray and are trying to raise funds for a home for teenage mothers and their babies. Of course these aren't things we could have ever done single-handedly; we've had a lot of support, both financial and practical, from local people and organizations.

One of the amazing things about long-term missionary work is that you really get to know the people and the culture so much more than if you just visit for a short time. We're really enjoying building relationships and growing to love people we would never have otherwise met. Of course, we've missed our friends and family. God has given us grace for that, but to be honest it's still been hard at times, particularly now that we are expecting our first child, a time when you really value being close to those you love. But we are committed to being here for as long as God calls us.

We're totally dependent on God from a financial point of view, both to clothe and feed ourselves and for the work we want to do in Kenya, but He has been very faithful to us even when the situation has seemed hopeless. It's a truth we all know—that God is able to do miracles if we put ourselves in the position where we need them!

We would definitely encourage anyone who's thinking about mission work of this kind to forget the nerves and just go for it! It's easy to look at ourselves and see our weaknesses, so we find it helps to remember that many of the people in the Bible thought they weren't up to the task, but God used them regardless. We've found that the most important skills to develop are to be humble and to come ready to serve and to learn. Make sure you have a strong group of friends who will pray for you and with you and who can give you good advice. Although it's not always easy, it is so exciting to step out and take a risk on God, to try things that we know will fail unless He turns up. If you're thinking of doing it, then keep asking God to open doors and show you where to go, what to do and how to do it.

If you think God may be calling you to this kind of missionary work, then chat and pray it through with trusted friends and leaders. Prepare yourself as much as possible by researching the place you are going to and talking to others who have walked a similar path.

Bless Your Local Town

Of course, you don't have to go abroad to get involved. For most of us there are plenty of people in our hometown who need help and support in some area of their lives.

A few years ago, Taryn, a member of our church, had a vision for setting up a pregnancy crisis center. She was passionate about supporting young girls who found themselves in the frightening position of being pregnant when they hadn't planned to be. Taryn was desperate that these women should have somewhere to go and someone to turn to who would love and support them and provide a listening ear. Many others in the church caught the vision and the center now runs not only a crisis pregnancy counseling service but also a mums and tots group for the teenage girls as well as a drop-in center where they can get support, access the Internet to apply for jobs and benefits, receive clothes and goods for their babies, and hang out and form relationships with others who are in a similar position.

Like this organization, another that I've always admired is XLP, a charity that works in its local area (the southeast boroughs of London) aiming to meet the social, educational and behavioral needs of young people. This involves everything from running school assemblies and homework and lunchtime/after-school clubs to literacy support and music and dance lessons. XLP works hard to show God's love to young people in a culturally relevant way, through building relationships and working with community groups, local authorities, local police and churches to provide the practical help needed in an area. Many of the young people it helps have achieved little at school, have few ambitions and are known as troublemakers. What they desperately need is someone to give them a helping hand, invest in them rather than write them off, and help them improve their lives—exactly what XLP aims to do.

Every town, city and village is different, so see what the need is in your area and match it up with things you're passionate about and able to do. There may be a volunteer bureau that will give you some ideas and put you in touch with various groups that need an extra pair of hands. You could visit people in hospitals and prisons, visit the elderly who may not get to see another smiling face all week, or offer to help out with a trust for homeless people. There are currently more needs than people to meet them, so whatever your gifts there's sure to be a way you can use them to bless others in your community.

Start in Your Local Church

Someone once told me that if you want to know the theology of any church, you should look at its architecture. If in the center there is a big pulpit decorated with a huge golden eagle, you can easily conclude that teaching is key to that church; or if the altar table seems the most visible thing, it may be a Catholic church, where Communion is key. In other places, like our church, we have wires and amps all over the place, so it's easy to tell that we place a priority on worship music.

If you have visited Soul Survivor Watford over the last few years, you will have noticed that we have a large black bin in front of the stage. You might think this is an odd and unsightly choice, but we use it as part of our worship. As we sing a song and come forward to put money in the offering baskets, we also encourage people to bring items of food and other useful goods to put in the bin to be distributed by our local social services team. This is such a simple way to bless our community. While doing the weekly shopping, it's easy to put in a few extra tins of food or some diapers and know that these will bless a local family struggling to put food on the table. The big black bin may look ugly, but it's a practical reminder to us of the poor and helps us to remember that our worship doesn't stop with singing.

There are so many needs everywhere we look, and there are so many things we can do about those needs. We all have different hearts, different amounts of time, different resources and talents. The point is that we're all called to do something. I know that I want to build things into my life that I can do on an ongoing basis so that my heart is continually being stretched and changed. As I've written this chapter and thought again about some of the different ways to get involved, I've felt challenged to make the fight for justice a part of my daily walk, as vital as prayer and praise as an expression of my relationship with God.

Why not stop for a few moments and think about what you have just read? Are there any areas that particularly excited you? There may be some things you are already doing, like giving regularly to charity, and some that can be built into your daily life quite easily and quickly, like praying. There may be other things you need to spend some time thinking and praying about to consider making them a reality.

Talk to your friends and family. See what you can do together and find people who share your desire to serve God in this way so that you can keep one another accountable and encouraged on the journey. Let's not leave this to other people, like the celebrities who are currently flying the flag for justice. This is something that we are all capable of getting involved in. We can make a real difference to this world, no matter how small our steps seem.

"And God is able to make all grace abound to you, so that in all things at all times, having all that you need, you will abound in every good work" (2 Cor. 9:8).

Further Information

Child Sponsorship
Visit www.compassion.com or www.actionaid.org.uk or www.worldvision.org.uk.

Charitable Gifts
Try www.greatgifts.org or www.oxfamunwrapped.com.

Fair Trade
See the campaigning section of www.tearfund.org for more details on Fair Trade products or visit www.maketradefair.com for more information.

Being an Ethical Consumer

Visit www.youth.tearfund.org and see their Lift the Label campaign (you can download a copy of their *Ethical Directory*) or buy the *Lift the Label* book by David Westlake and Esther Stansfield. This includes information about investing your money wisely.

Mission Work

A good place to start for short-term missions is www.christian-vocations.org, which has advice, vacancies and resources, including a short-term service directory that you can order. Tearfund has long- and short-term missions vacancies advertised on their website for both the UK and overseas (www.tearfund.org/jobseekers).

How Do They All Work Together?

Love and Action

The greatest of these is love.
1 Corinthians 13:13

I have to confess that when I became a youth worker at St. Andrew's Chorleywood, there were times when I thought I was quite important. Before, during and after services, I could be seen rushing around feeling very busy and significant. One day, when I was in the midst of my work, an elderly lady from the congregation called to me as I went past, "Mike, won't you come and sit down for a minute?"

I sighed heavily and looked at my watch, hoping to convey with that and a raised eyebrow how very precious my time was and that she was keeping me from my work.

"Come on, Mike," she encouraged. So I dutifully sat, willing her to be quick. "Don't you just love Jesus, Mike?" she asked

quietly, a look of such pleasure on her face. "Doesn't it make you so happy to know Him and to know He loves you?"

I'm sure I looked surprised; I'd been expecting a half-hour lecture on varicose veins.

"Any time you're passing by, pop in and see me; the door's always open and I'd love to pray and worship Jesus with you."

I was truly humbled. There I was, thinking that I was so busy and important serving Jesus, and what Hilda wanted to do was talk about how much she loved Him. She had chosen what was better—not to rush around hoping to impress God and others with acts of service, but to love God with all her heart and to let that love overflow in her life. The truth was that there was an aroma about Hilda, and no, it wasn't that she'd forgotten to wash. Paul said, "For we are to God the aroma of Christ among those who are being saved and those who are perishing" (2 Cor. 2:15). Hilda stank strongly, not as I did of hard work and self-importance, but of the fragrance of Christ.

Whenever I'm tempted to put serving God before my relationship with Him, I remember Hilda and her wonderful friendship with her heavenly Father. I remember that it's easy to get caught up in the busyness—after all, haven't we just been looking at the great needs around us and some of the things we can do to try and address them? But we have to remember that the very first and therefore greatest commandment is to "Love the Lord your God with all your heart and with all your soul and with all your mind and with all your strength" (Mark 12:30). Jesus didn't say, "*Serve* the Lord your God with all your heart." He used the word "love." We often get busy with the serving bit and then love God from the worn-out dregs of what's left over.

Richard Foster says in *Celebration of Discipline*, "Service flows out of worship. Service instead of worship is idolatry."[1] It's easy to fill our time and not make space to meet with God, but we mustn't replace our relationship with God with acts of service in His name. As Foster points out, this is sin. Even Jesus, in all He did while on Earth, regularly made hanging out with His Father a priority. It would be extreme arrogance to think that if Jesus could afford to take time out from what He was doing to spend it with His Father, then anything we are doing is more important than doing the same.

We see God's heart on this in Revelation 2, where He commends the church in Ephesus for persevering and enduring hardships in His name; but there's something not quite right: "Yet I hold this against you: You have forsaken your first love" (v. 4). The most important thing for us to remember is that we must put our love for God first. As Paul said, "If I give all I possess to the poor and surrender my body to the flames, but have not love, I gain nothing" (1 Cor. 13:3).

The familiar story of Mary's extravagant act of worship highlights that worship is our first priority. When Jesus was having dinner with friends, Mary poured over His feet expensive perfume worth about the equivalent of a year's wages. Although Judas had ulterior motives (to steal the money for himself), he asked a valid question: Wouldn't it have been better to have sold the perfume and given the money to the poor rather than "wasting" it on Jesus? Given what we've seen of God's heart for the poor, wouldn't Jesus agree with Judas? Not at all. Jesus said, "You will always have the poor among you, but you will not always have me" (John 12:8).

Actions Demonstrate Genuine Love

Love is the most important thing; and the truth is, it's pretty much impossible to love God and not love others. Saint Augustine said, "Love God and do what you like." He knew that to love God means to grow to become like Him and to share His heart, so "what we like" starts to fall in line with what God wants. When we put worship first, the other things should fall into place. James addresses this issue of our actions going hand in hand with our faith and relationship with God:

> Dear friends, do you think you'll get anywhere in this if you learn all the right words but never do anything? Does merely talking about faith indicate that a person really has it? For instance, you come upon an old friend dressed in rags and half-starved and say, "Good morning, friend! Be clothed in Christ! Be filled with the Holy Spirit!" and walk off without providing so much as a coat or a cup of soup—where does that get you? Isn't it obvious that God-talk without God-acts is outrageous nonsense? I can already hear one of you agreeing by saying, "Sounds good. You take care of the faith department, I'll handle the works department." Not so fast. You can no more show me your works apart from your faith than I can show you my faith apart from my works. Faith and works, works and faith, fit together hand in glove (Jas. 2:14-18, *THE MESSAGE*).

James goes so far as to say that if you try to divide your faith and your works, you "end up with a corpse on your hands" because "faith expresses itself in works." Acts of kindness toward other people, whether helping a friend or sending money to someone overseas that you've never met before, are first and foremost acts of love and devotion to God.

In the Gospel of Matthew, we read the story Jesus tells of the Day of Judgment. He says that all the nations will be before Him and He will separate them into two categories: the sheep and the goats. To the sheep on His right-hand side He will say:

"Come, you who are blessed by my Father; take your inheritance, the kingdom prepared for you since the creation of the world. For I was hungry and you gave me something to eat, I was thirsty and you gave me something to drink, I was a stranger and you invited me in, I needed clothes and you clothed me, I was sick and you looked after me, I was in prison and you came to visit me." Then the righteous will answer him, "Lord, when did we see you hungry and feed you, or thirsty and give you something to drink? When did we see you a stranger and invite you in, or needing clothes and clothe you? When did we see you sick or in prison and go to visit you?" The King will reply, "I tell you the truth, whatever you did for one of the least of these brothers of mine, you did for me" (Matt. 25:34-40).

The sheep didn't even recognize what they were doing. They looked after the stranger and the hungry without realizing that

God saw each and every act and accepted it as love and devotion for Himself.

The goats on His left-hand side, however, hear a very different story. They are told that they did not love God in looking after the homeless and the prisoner, so they must depart from God's presence for eternity.

Every act of kindness for someone in need, whether intended or not, is first and foremost an act of love for Jesus. It's not about being able to say that we've done our quota of good deeds or trying to hook people in. We are called to love because God loves; we are called to give because God gives; we are called to be merciful because God is merciful.

We're not trying to earn God's love, approval or favor through our works: "For it is by grace you have been saved, through faith—and this not from yourselves, it is the gift of God—not by works, so that no-one can boast" (Eph. 2:8-9). The deeds don't save us or make us right with God, but they are outward signs that we know we are saved and have received God's love. Because of Him, we can't help but love others.

What Happens When You Separate Worship, Evangelism and Justice?

Worship without justice. We've seen that worship is to be the top priority, but what happens if we do this but don't seek justice for the poor? We see God's view of this in Amos 5 when He rebuked His people:

> I hate, I despise your religious feasts;
> I cannot stand your assemblies.

Even though you bring me burnt offerings and grain
offerings,
I will not accept them.
Though you bring choice fellowship offerings,
I will have no regard for them.
Away with the noise of your songs!
I will not listen to the music of your harps.
But let justice roll on like a river,
righteousness like a never-failing stream!
(Amos 5:21–24).

Of course, God wasn't objecting to the feasts and the offerings in and of themselves; it was the heart attitude behind them. These people were living it up at the expense of the poor. While they were religiously offering their tithes and sacrifices, they were corrupt and dishonest in their business practices—court judges were being bribed and they were oppressing the poor. God will not stand for hypocrisy. What He makes clear here is that if our actions do not back up our words, then the words mean nothing. God doesn't hide from us what He wants us to do; it's not a guessing game that we may or may not get right. He spells it out: I want justice; I want your actions to back up your words.

Spiritual and secular combined. Our culture often separates the spiritual from the secular, and so we lead what would be called a dualistic lifestyle. The Hebrews understood that we are made up of body, mind and spirit, and they saw all these elements working together as one. For example, we've seen worship as something we do on a Sunday at church, whereas it should be expressed in each area of our life and society.

So much of what we do in church is inaccessible to those who are unchurched. It doesn't mean anything to them, so it's not easy for them to come and be a part of it. We have to look at all areas of our lives and see how we can build bridges with those who are outside of the church.

Over the last few years it has troubled me that most of the creativity in music, art and drama in today's culture comes from outside the church. This can't be right, as those of us in relationship with God have the Creator's spirit inside of us. The Holy Spirit is the spirit of creativity, but so often it seems as though we're not willing to take risks in creativity because we're afraid of making mistakes. We need to be released and to release others to go on an adventure.

If we play it safe, we'll sit in our pews doing what we've always done, and we'll pass on the same cautiousness to generation after generation. It's a big challenge to make our music contemporary and culturally relevant. In my opinion the best worship music would be a Christian version of Simon and Garfunkel or, if we really wanted to be cutting edge, Meatloaf! This generation doesn't share my tastes in music—a tragedy in my opinion, but I'm trying to deal with it.

I've come across lots of young Christian musicians who feel trapped and constricted. They have two passions, worship and evangelism, and they have been made to feel as though they have to choose which route to take. I think it is desperately important for the growth of the Church that we release people to realize that they don't have to choose and that both can and should work together. Many have been bound by the fear that they are being "worldly" in their desire to take their music outside of the church, when this is in fact what God has called them to do. We need to ask God to forgive us for the times when our attitudes and fears have held people back, even if our intentions have been good. We also need to ask forgiveness for those times when we have misunderstood God's call on other people's lives.

Christians who have spearheaded the way toward culturally relevant music range from Kevin Prosch to Delirious? and Onehundredhours. They've all had different approaches and have forced us to question what worship is, what performance is and how to use them both to glorify God's name.

However, it would be ridiculous to think that we need to take only creativity in music out from the church and into the world. This should be about all areas and all gifts. Whether we have a talent for sculpture, creating websites, creative writing or acting, we need to see these talents as an expression of worship and invite the Holy Spirit to come into those areas, bless those gifts and increase them, and use them for His name.

We've seen it throughout history with poets such as Gerard Manley Hopkins and Christina Rossetti, who proclaimed Christ through their writings, and from classic novels like *Pilgrim's Progress* to the *Chronicles of Narnia*, which are being born again in a series of films for this generation. We must use our creativity and all of our gifts to declare God's name and nature, as this is both part of our worship and part of our evangelism.

Where does the Church fit in? Often the Church has attached itself to particular party agendas—when we speak up for unborn babies' rights, we are following a traditionally right-wing agenda, and when we campaign for countries suffering from debts imposed on them by Western nations, we take on a left-wing agenda. But it has to be about more than falling on this side or that. We must stand up for ecology as well as personal freedom; we want to free people from living under dictatorship as well as make sure that we do not rape the planet. As we get involved with fighting for the poor and bringing a biblical agenda to society, we will begin to have a voice again.

But we can't merely talk about these problems and issues. We have to be a positive part of the solution, and we have a great opportunity because governments are realizing that the cost of healthcare and education is prohibitive; thus, they're inviting the Church to play a role as it did in previous years. We must not miss this opportunity to play our part, to reconnect with society in a way we haven't done in the past 200 years.

Sometimes we have to *be* good news before we earn the right to *preach* the good news. This is true for all our friendships and relationships—we want to be a blessing and not just talk about God's blessings—but it's also true if we want people in the wider community to become Christians.

What Happens When You Bring Worship, Evangelism and Justice Together?

Some years ago, Steve Chalke spoke at Soul Survivor. As he preached, he challenged us as part of our worship to go out of the meeting hall, back to our tents and to return with an item of clothing we would like to offer to God to be taken to homeless people in London. The idea was not to bring something we didn't really need or want anymore, but to sacrifice something we had brought with us, not realizing this would be asked of us. Steve asked that we worship as we went to collect our donations as a reminder that this was another expression of our love for God.

So the band continued to play as 6,000 kids filed from the meeting room back to their tents. Gradually the empty hall began to fill up again and huge queues formed outside by the truck as the young people offered their clothes and belongings. Some cried as they gave over the things they valued, and all the while songs of love and devotion were being sung. All of a sudden it hit me that this was an amazing expression of worship that Steve had challenged us to offer, and this seemed to me to be the worship God required: not only to sing the songs of devotion but to mean them so much that we would be willing to put that love into action and sacrifice whatever He asked of us.

Of course, this expression of worship wasn't without its issues (some parents weren't exactly thrilled to find out their children had given away birthday presents, and we were surprised at how many kids "gave" items that didn't belong to them), but the majority of people there gave something they loved as a token of their devotion to God.

This was an act of worship to God; it was evangelism, because every person on the streets of London who received a new pair of running shoes or a warm sweater knew it came from Christians. And it was an act of justice to share what we had with others in need.

Being Good News

In 2004, we ran "Soul in the City," where 11,600 young people descended on London to love and serve those who live and work there. It was a worship festival in that we worshiped in song each morning and evening, and then worshiped on the streets during the days. This worship took many shapes and forms, from gardening projects, painting over graffiti, and decorating youth and community centers, to running holiday clubs for children.

The idea was to serve people with no strings attached—there was no condition that we would do something for them if they would only listen to a five-minute presentation of the gospel or come to an event we were putting on. But what happens when you offer something for nothing? People want to know why. The last thing the city of London expected was for more than 10,000 young people to come and pay to serve them for nothing. We couldn't get away from talking about Jesus, because our actions caused people to ask questions. They wanted to know what would make a young person in today's self-centered culture give up part of his or her summer holiday and pay for the privilege of clearing up the litter of complete strangers who live hundreds of miles away. There was no other answer people could give—there was only one reason we were doing this: Jesus. We found that people were much more open to hearing about Jesus once they'd seen Him in action. We could say that Jesus loved them because we'd demonstrated it.

We estimated that 6,000 people made commitments to Jesus through the various projects. Lasting change was brought to communities, smiles were put on people's faces, hope was put back in people's hearts and many thousands were left with a lasting impression of young people serving in the name of Jesus. Not rattling a collection tin in His name. Not someone preaching at them and telling them they were sinners—just the people of God loving and serving.

The Key to Revival

It can't just be about the one-time mission. This has to form part of our daily life. If we want to see revival, we need to bring all these elements of worship, evangelism and justice together, realizing that a life of passionate worship of God means first and foremost spending time with Him, loving Him and growing in our relationship with Him, as well as feeding the hungry, standing up for those who suffer injustice, identifying with them in their pain and suffering, and being willing to stand alongside them and fight on their behalf. We should be preaching the gospel at all times, speaking and acting out God's love to a hurt and broken world.

We have to realize that to tell people about Jesus while leaving them starving to death or wasting away in prison when they have been falsely accused is offensive to God. Equally, to meet their physical needs and ignore their spiritual needs is appalling, as whatever improvement we can hope to bring to their life on Earth is nothing in comparison to being reconciled with their heavenly Father.

It's unlikely to be a glamorous task. The vast majority of us will never have films made about our lives, enter a room to rapturous applause, be followed by a news crew or be asked for our autograph at the end of a day's work. God never promised us any of those things. As we fix our eyes on Him, we remember that while there is a place for big dreams and wild adventures, worshiping God is about making good choices every day, even in the seemingly small decisions we make.

What God did say is that He would see each act we do in His name and that He would notice each good choice we make. It may be that no one on Earth ever knows all that you do in the name of Jesus, but when you stand before your heavenly Father, you will be sure to hear the words "Well done, good and faithful servant"(Matt. 25:21).

Therefore I urge you, brothers [and sisters] in Christ, in view of God's overwhelming love and mercy, to offer your bodies [your hearts, your minds, your voices, your hands, your feet, your bank accounts, your shopping decisions, your Internet access, your homes and your possessions] as living sacrifices [to do with as He will]. For this is a holy and pleasing spiritual act of worship to the Lord your God (adapted from Romans 12:1).

Chapter Two: The Worship God Requires

1. Tim Hughes, "When the Tears Fall," copyright © 2003 Thankyou Music. Administered by worshiptogether.com songs excluding UK and Europe, administered by kingswaysongs.com, tym@kingsway.co.uk. Used by permission.

Chapter Three: Worship as a Lifestyle

1. David Ruis, *The Worship God Is Seeking* (Ventura, CA: Regal Books, 2004).
2. Brother Lawrence, trans. by E. M. Blaiklock, *The Practice of the Presence of God* (London: Hodder & Stoughton, 1981).
3. Richard Foster, *Celebration of Discipline* (London: Hodder & Stoughton, 1989).

Chapter Seven: God's Heart for Justice

1. Gary A. Haugen, *Good News About Injustice: A Witness of Courage in a Hurting World* (Downers Grove, IL: InterVarsity Press, 1999).

Chapter Eight: Compassion for a Broken World

1. Andrew Simms, "Selling Suicide—Farming, False Promises and Genetic Engineering in Developing Countries," May 1999. http://www.christian-aid.org.uk/indepth/9905suic/suicide1.htm (accessed January 2007).
2. "Worldwide HIV and AIDS Statistics: Global HIV/AIDS Estimates, End of 2006," UNAIDS/World Health Organization data. http://www.avert.org/worldstats.htm (accessed January 2007).
3. "Joint Report Details Escalating Global Orphans Crisis Due to AIDS: Number of Children Orphaned by AIDS Will Increase Dramatically," U.S. Agency for International Development Press Release, July 10, 2002. http://www.usaid.gov/press/releases/2002/pr020710.html (accessed January 2007).
4. "More and Better Aid: In More Detail," MakePovertyHistory.org. http://www.makepovertyhistory.org/whatwewant/aid.shtml (accessed January 2007).
5. Anup Shaw, "The Scale of the Debt Crisis," July 2, 2005, data from "World Bank Global Finance Development 1999 Report." http://www.globalissues.org/TradeRelated/Debt/Scale.asp (accessed January 2007).
6. "Opportunities for Africa's Newborns," The Partnership for Maternal, Newborn and Child Health, World Health Organization, 2007. http://www.who.int/pmnch/media/publications/en/ (accessed January 2007).
7. "Water: Funky Facts," Global Gang, Christian Aid website. http://www.globalgang.org.uk/homeworkhelp/water/ (accessed January 2007).
8. Anup Shaw, "Poverty Facts and Stats," November 24, 2006, data from "Unicef State of the World's Children 2005 Report." http://www.globalissues.org/TradeRelated/Facts.asp#fact26 (accessed January 2007).
9. "Managing More than Most: A Statistical Analysis of Families with Sick or Disabled Children," Contact a Family, 2007, data from "2001 Census Special License Household Sample of Anonymised Records." http://www.cafamily.org.uk/campaignsManagingMore.pdf (accessed January 2007).

10. "Facts and Figures About Child Abuse," NSPCC, data from "Home Office (2004) Crime in England and Wales 2002-3: Supplementary Volume 1, Homicide and Gun Crime." http://www.nspcc.org.uk/whatwedo/mediacentre/mediaresources/facts_and_figures_wda33295.html (accessed January 2007).
11. "Mind Factsheet: Attempted Suicide," National Association for Mental Health, 1998. http://www.mind.org.uk/Information/Factsheets/Suicide/#_ftnref60 (accessed January 2007).
12. Ibid.
13. Michka Assayas, *Bono: In Conversation with Michka Assayas* (London: Hodder & Stoughton, 2005).

Chapter Nine: What Can I Do?
1. Richard Foster, *Celebration of Discipline* (London: Hodder & Stoughton, 1980, 1989), n.p.
2. Pete Greig and Dave Roberts, *Red Moon Rising: The Story of 24-7 Prayer* (Lake Mary, FL: Relevant Media Group Inc., 2003), n.p.
3. www.corporatewatch.org.uk (accessed January 2006).

Epilogue: How Do They All Work Together?
1. Richard Foster, *Celebration of Discipline* (London: Hodder & Stoughton, 1980, 1989), n.p.

BIBLIOGRAPHY

Assayas, Michka. *Bono: In Conversation with Michka Assayas.* London: Hodder & Stoughton, 2005.

Foster, Richard. *Celebration of Discipline.* London: Hodder & Stoughton, 1980, 1989.

Greig, Pete and Dave Roberts. *Red Moon Rising: The Story of 24-7 Prayer.* Lake Mary, FL: Relevant Media Group Inc., 2003.

Haugen, Gary A. *Good News About Injustice: A Witness of Courage in a Hurting World.* Downers Grove, IL: InterVarsity Press, 1999.

Lawrence, Brother. *The Practice of the Presence of God.* Trans. E.M. Blaiklock. London: Hodder & Stoughton, 1981.

Ruis, David. *The Worship God Is Seeking.* Ventura, CA: Regal Books, 2004.

OTHER BOOKS BY MIKE PILAVACHI

Soul Survivor
Finding Passion and Purpose in the Dry Places

For the Audience of One
Worshiping the One and Only in Everything You Do

Life Beneath the Surface
Thoughts on a Deeper Spiritual Life

More Ways to Seek Justice

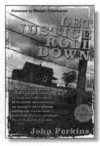